SOCCER STARS ON THE PITCH

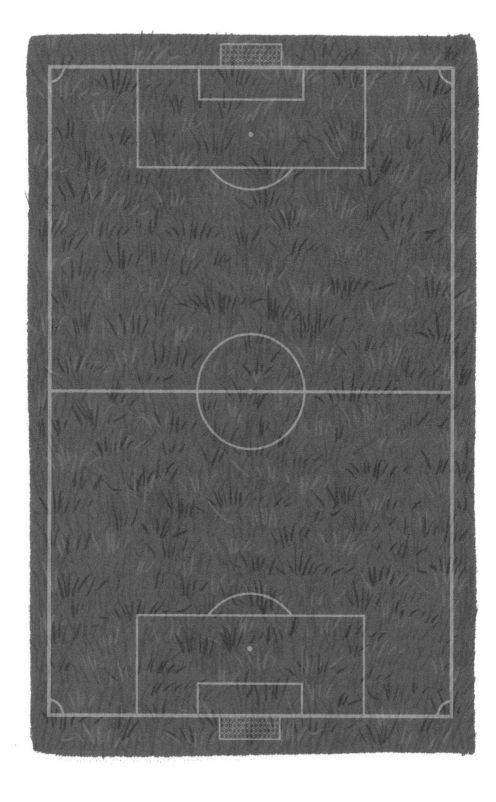

SOCCER STARS

ON THE PITCH

Biographies of Today's Best Players

TANYA KEITH

Illustrations by
BRENNA DAUGHERTY

ROCKRIDGE
PRESS

Interior and Cover Designer: Eric Pratt
Art Producer: Sue Bischofberger
Editor: David Lytle
Production Editor: Mia Moran

Illustrations © Brenna Daugherty, 2019 • brennadaugherty.com
Author photo © Doug Jotzke

ISBN: Print 978-1-64611-212-8 | eBook 978-1-64611-063-6

R0

To my husband, Doug, and our Hat Trick of Children: Aviva (the Korea baby), Raphael (the "I will not be pregnant at the Germany World Cup" baby), and Iolana (the absolute best souvenir I can possibly imagine from the Brazil World Cup). Thank you for being the best travelers I could ever imagine, and for supporting me through writing this book.

CONTENTS

Introduction

Twenty-five years ago, I fell in love with soccer at the World Cup and decided to spend my life following the beautiful game around the world.

Soccer has always been my opportunity to travel and learn about the world—sometimes by airplane, and sometimes from the comfort of my couch by tuning into games happening on the other side of the world.

My obsession with soccer began long before the Internet made it easy to be a part of this global passion. We used to wait for our *Soccer America* magazine to arrive in the mailbox, and we'd have to hunt down a game with a satellite dish if it wasn't available on cable. Now, of course, anyone with an Internet connection can follow teams large and small, track players on social media, watch games streaming online, and interact with supporters groups.

It's an exciting time to be a soccer fan.

Over the past quarter century, I have traveled to 10 World Cups, seen exciting games in a dozen different countries, and met some incredible people. To top it off, I've been lucky enough to have my three kids share some of those adventures with me. Now, I'm writing this book to share my love of soccer with people everywhere.

People of all ages regularly ask me to adopt them so they can travel with my family on our adventures; this book is a close as I can get to including as many people as possible on a family-friendly budget.

I hope through reading this book, you'll learn about some great soccer players and be inspired to find something you love and pursue it with all your heart.

THE PLAYERS: WHY THEY WERE PICKED

This book is a fantasy league team of the best players around the world as goalkeepers, defenders, midfielders, and forwards. Of course, "the best" is subjective, and my choices were influenced by my desire to take you on a journey around the world and introduce you to as many leagues and regions as possible. You'll also find brief honorable mention player bios for each position, as well as stories of legendary players who changed the game of soccer and helped create the modern sport as it exists today.

There are many ways I could have chosen players for this book. I have my personal favorites, naturally, and there are outstanding players of any given day, week, month, or year. Rather than do it on my own, though, I got some help from an expert—my son's most soccer-obsessed buddy, thirteen-year-old Jonah.

Jonah gave me a great starting 11, and, from there, I looked for players who are up-and-coming in their league. I tried to represent as many countries, regions, and leagues as I could, and there are many more interesting and worthy players in the game today than can fit in this book. If I left your favorite player off the final list, I'm truly sorry. I left off a few of my own favorites, too. I hope you'll find at least one player in these pages who inspires you to further your soccer passion and learning.

Finally, I am writing this book during the 2019 Women's World Cup, and I am here to proclaim that the women who are playing soccer today are mind-blowingly cool, strong, fierce, and absolutely worthy of their own entire book, hopefully soon to follow this one. These women have followed their passion for soccer despite the limits of financial reward for their efforts, and I find so many of their stories so inspiring.

A NOTE ON TERMINOLOGY

I am an American, and we call the sport *soccer*; however, most of the world calls this beautiful game *football*. I use *soccer* almost exclusively throughout this book, but I did maintain *football* in things like titles of European Championships. Whether you call it soccer, football, footie, fussball, futebol, or anything else, I think we can agree that it's the greatest game in the world.

HUGO LLORIS

Hugo
LLORIS

★ ★ ★

1

POSITION: GOALIE
CLUB TEAM: TOTTENHAM HOTSPUR F.C.,
PREMIER LEAGUE
NATIONAL TEAM: FRANCE
HEIGHT: 6'2" – **WEIGHT:** 172 LBS
BORN: DECEMBER 26, 1986

⚽ WORLD CUP WINNER, 2018
⚽ FRENCH CUP WINNER,
    11/12 OLYMPIQUE LYON
⚽ EUROPEAN U19 CHAMPION 2015
⚽ FRENCH SUPER CUP WINNER
    12/13 OLYMPIQUE LYON

$

TRANSFERMARKT 2019 ESTIMATED VALUE:

28.5 MILLION

 @iamhugolloris

H ugo Lloris was born in Nice (pronounced like "niece"), a midsized city on the Mediterranean coast in Southern France. His mother was a lawyer, his father a banker, and his younger brother, Gautier, would also grow up to be a professional soccer player.

Soccer was not Lloris's first love; he preferred tennis, developing into a highly ranked youth player. Soccer was just what he and his friends played for fun during down time at tennis practice. However, at Centre de Diffusion et d'Action Culturelle (CEDAC), a French community center where local kids play sports, the coaches saw a young Lloris playing soccer and asked him to join their team. Although Lloris's parents were initially unhappy about this addition to his schedule, they finally allowed him to join the soccer team as long as he kept up with his tennis and schoolwork.

Lloris tried several positions while playing at CEDAC until his coaches noticed his ball-handling skills and realized he could make an excellent goalkeeper. In a 2017 interview with *Diario AS*, Lloris said he liked the responsibility of being in the net, but he also quipped, "I don't know why I wanted to be a goalkeeper, either; maybe because I could throw myself at the feet of my opponents, for the risk."

Once he settled into the role of keeper, his talents were discovered by Dominique Baratelli, the goalkeeper for Olympique Gymnaste Club Nice Côte d'Azur (OGC Nice). Baratelli, who also played on the French national team, recommended that ten-year-old Lloris join OGC Nice's youth program.

At that time, Lloris decided to quit playing tennis. "I had to choose," he said, "because at that age [soccer teams] ask you to go and train five times a week and play during the weekends, and it was impossible to continue playing tennis."

Lloris developed his skills at OGC Nice's Youth Academy, and, by the 2003–04 season, he led the club's under-17 (U17) team to the championship of France's national league competition for youth clubs—the Championnat Nationaux des 18 ans. His success as the starting keeper in that tournament earned him a promotion to reserve keeper in the French fourth division for the following season.

A SWEEPER KEEPER TO LIGUE 1

Just one year later, Lloris was called up to Ligue 1, France's top professional soccer division, and was OGC Nice's starting goalkeeper for the club's Coupe de la Ligue games. His professional debut was on October 25, 2005, at just shy of nineteen years old, when he earned a shutout (allowed no goals) over LB Châteauroux. He continued in the net through the final (the club's first appearance in the final), keeping CS Sedan Ardennes scoreless and helping his club upset favorites FC Girondins de Bordeaux and AS Monaco FC, but, ultimately, OGC Nice lost to AS Nancy in the final 2 to 1.

Because all those appearances were in a tournament, Lloris's first league game wasn't until March 18, 2006, when Nice played Nancy once again. This time, he held them scoreless for a 1 to 0 victory. He had only four appearances the remainder of the season, but, the following year, he started all but one game. Over the entire season, he allowed a mere 36 goals—a number that was only beaten by three other much more experienced keepers in the league.

Lloris faced a recurring injury throughout the early 2007-08 season but recovered in time to play most of the season. When he was fit, he was racking up big wins, allowing only 24 goals in 30 games and keeping 13 clean sheets (yet another way to say he allowed no goals). His performance attracted the attention of several top league teams, including AC Milan and Tottenham Hotspur, but he selected Olympique Lyonnais in the city of Lyon because they promised him the starting goalkeeper position. The trade went through for a reported €8.5 million transfer fee.

His first year at Lyon was an exciting one right from his first game, a 3 to 0 win against Toulouse FC. He allowed only 27 goals in league play, nabbed

Goalkeeper of the Year honors, and was named to the league's Team of the Year. In September of his second season, he won the UNFP's Player of the Month award. He also came in third that season for *France Football* magazine's French Player of the Year.

In 2009, the UEFA Champions League pitted Lyon and Lloris against Real Madrid C.F. and superstar forward, Cristiano Ronaldo, in the knockout round. He was able to get a fingertip on a Ronaldo shot, saving the day for a 1 to 0 Lyon victory. He later faced Ronaldo again in a 1 to 1 draw that qualified Lyon for the quarterfinals. That one goal he allowed in? It was a sixth-minute goal by Ronaldo— the first goal scored on Lloris in over 620 minutes of play! A week later, Lloris scored his second UNFP Ligue 1 Goalkeeper of the Year honors in a row.

The 2010–11 season proved to be a transition point for Lloris. He became frustrated that Lyon was not playing to the high standards he set for himself. After one particularly disappointing match against his former club, Nice, Lloris went on a cursing streak in the locker room. "It was a human reaction," he later explained. "There was frustration and accumulation and it had to come out."

Tottenham Hotspur signed Lloris on August 31, 2012, to the tune of €10 million and a €5 million variable, with Lyon retaining 20 percent of Lloris's

future transfer profits. In the United States, we have a pay-to-play soccer program, where parents pay to have their kids play soccer. In many other countries, clubs recruit players to play for them; if a player makes it big, that club makes money off the player by way of transfer fees, which is essentially selling the rights to that player. Many people think this is a better way of bringing players into the system because it allows players from all income levels a chance to play.

On November 3, 2013, during his second season with Tottenham, Lloris got a scare when he was knocked unconscious after a collision with Everton F.C.'s forward, Romelu Lukaku. Unfortunately, concussion protocols were not what they are today, and Lloris convinced his coaches to allow him to continue playing. At the time, his coach said, "The saves he did after the incident proved [the decision to allow him to continue] right." However, by today's standards, he would have been subbed out to protect him from potential brain injury.

Switching to Tottenham required that Lloris adapt his style to his new league. "In England there is a lot of contact in the box, a lot of quality crosses," he said in an interview with *Guardian* journalist, Jonathan Wilson. "Here, the keeper is less protected than in France or in European competitions. I have gone on working as I did in France but adapting to the different approach of the keeper's position." His adaptations inspired Wilson to give him the nickname, "The Sweeper Keeper," as Lloris took on duties of keeper and sweeper—a defender that sweeps the ball out of the defense as opposed to man-marking.

A NATIONAL TEAM CAREER ON A ROCKET

Lloris has also had an outstanding career with the French Men's National Team. He started on the French National Youth Team, debuting at age seventeen in a friendly match against Germany in March 2004. His national team career launched like a rocket; he played all five matches that led to France winning the 2005 European U19 Football Championship. His time on the U21 team was short-lived, however, because he was already getting called up to the senior national team.

His first official cap (appearance) for France was November 19, 2008, in a scoreless game against Uruguay. He helped France qualify for the 2010 FIFA World Cup in a home-and-away series with Ireland that earned him the nickname, "Saint Lloris." He played for France in all three opening-round games, but France did not advance past the group stage that year.

Starting in November following the 2010 World Cup, Lloris began captaining the French side. They had appearances in both the UEFA Euro 2012 and the 2014 World Cup, getting sent home by the eventual champion in both cases (it may not be fun getting eliminated from a tournament, but if you have to go home, at least let it be to the champion).

Lloris's 100th cap came in the 2018 World Cup in France's second group stage game. France prevailed throughout the tournament to face Croatia in the final on July 15. It was an exciting, high-scoring game, including what broadcasters called one "moment of madness" when Lloris tried to be The Sweeper Keeper but had his pass cut off by Croatia's Mario Mandžukić, who immediately scored. Luckily for France, that was the final goal of a 4 to 2 match, allowing France to hoist its second World Cup trophy.

Shortly after his team's victory, Lloris was convicted of drunk driving in August 2018. In an interview with *The Telegram* following the incident, he spoke about how empty he felt after winning the 2018 World Cup. He took responsibility for drunk driving after the taxi he had called canceled, saying in a statement, "I wish to apologize wholeheartedly to my family, the club, my teammates, the manager, and all of the supporters. Drunk-driving is completely unacceptable, I take full responsibility for my actions, and it is not the example I wish to set."

Lloris married his childhood sweetheart, Marine, on July 6, 2012. She founded the children's wear line Manège en Sucre and has degrees in human resources and law. They have two daughters: Anna Rose, born on September 23, 2010, and Guiliana, born February 24, 2014.

FUN FACTS

⚽ Hugo Lloris developed his philosophy of life in the net: "A goalkeeper has to be humble because the next play is always the most difficult one."

⚽ Hugo's brother, Gautier Lloris, plays for Hugo's former club, OGC Nice.

⚽ Lloris was featured on the cover of the French version of the video game, *FIFA 11*.

⚽ If you want to see social media posts of Lloris's family, you can follow his wife, @llorismarine_off.

Honorable Mentions
GOALKEEPERS

TIM HOWARD

I'm obsessed with US goalkeepers, so I had to feature one here—and since Howard and I are both originally from northern New Jersey, he edged out Brad Friedel. Of course, he has a few other claims to fame besides his birth state.

Howard has played in both Major League Soccer (MLS) and the English Premiere League (EPL). During his 250th cap for Everton in England, he became the fourth goalkeeper to ever score a goal in an EPL match (videos of that incredible end-to-end goal are online and absolutely worth checking out).

Howard is also the most capped goalkeeper from the US Men's National Team (USMNT). He became famous as part of our "Cinderella story" at the 2009 Confederations Cup, when the team miraculously beat Spain in the semifinal and then held a lead over powerhouse Brazil in the final through the first half before Brazil eventually won 3 to 2. Howard won the Golden Glove award for the tournament's best keeper for his efforts.

He helped the USMNT reach the Round of 16 in both the 2010 and 2014 FIFA World Cups and stood on his head (metaphorically speaking) against Belgium in the USMNT's last game of the 2014 tournament. He made 15 saves in that game (a World Cup record), many of them completely brilliant—even by neutral standards. Although the USMNT lost that match 2 to 1 in overtime, Howard's dazzling performance, keeping it score-less for 90 minutes, spawned endless GIFs and memes in his honor.

If you want to learn more about Tim Howard, read his book, *The Keeper*, in which he talks about soccer and his life dealing with Tourette's syndrome and obsessive-compulsive disorder (OCD).

JAN OBLAK

Slovenian Jan Oblak is the son of a goalkeeper, and his big sister, Teja, plays for Slovenia's basketball team. As a ten year old, he left his club for the capital, Ljubljana. His professional debut came at age sixteen, when the team's keeper, Robert Volk, said, "This kid is better than me," and stepped aside. Too young to drive at the time, Oblak had to ride his bike 25 kilometers (about 15 miles) to get to practice.

Getting a call up to Slovenia's national U21 team at age seventeen attracted the attention of clubs across Europe. He signed with S.L. Benfica in 2010, which loaned him to several different clubs around Portugal until the 2013–14 season. That's when he began playing for Benfica and went on to win the Primeira Liga's Best Goalkeeper of the Year award.

He is currently playing for Atlético Madrid in Spain's La Liga and has more than 20 caps for Slovenia. In 2016, Oblak racked up an incredible 41 clean sheets over 68 games in all competitions. His performance inspired Enrique Cereza, Atlético president, to proclaim, "I think that if he's not the best goalkeeper in the world, he's the second best."

Gamechanger
RENÉ HIGUITA

If you haven't heard of René Higuita, let me introduce him with two words: scorpion kick.

That's the name of the move of epic greatness that Higuita came up with (there are photos of it online that you really must see to believe). A scorpion kick involves diving forward while kicking your feet out behind you toward the back of your head—like a scorpion's sting. Higuita's signature kick earned him the nickname "El Loco" (the madman) and is one of the reasons he is called "the craziest keeper in the history of football." It didn't hurt that he also looked the part, sporting brightly colored and wildly patterned jerseys long before it was popular.

His style of play was equally flamboyant. He was known for collecting the ball, taking off running out of his area, dribbling down the field, and sometimes scoring at the end of his run. In fact, with 41 career goals, he is the fourth highest-scoring goalkeeper in history.

But Higuita was more than just flashy. Because of Higuita's pioneering "sweeper-keeper" style in the 1990 World Cup, FIFA changed the *Laws of the Game* to state that keepers could not pick up a ball that had been passed back to them by their

own field players. When Higuita was asked about his legacy in a 2018 FIFA interview, he said, "It was only after people saw René Higuita play that way that the rules were changed. It was decided that goalkeepers had to play with their feet. You play the ball back to them now and they can't pick it up. Not even Pelé, Maradona, or Messi have achieved that."

REAL MADRID, LA LIGA

★ SERGIO RAMOS ★

Sergio RAMOS

★ ★ ★

7

POSITION: MIDFIELDER
CLUB TEAM: REAL MADRID C.F., LA LIGA
NATIONAL TEAM: SPAIN
HEIGHT: 6'0" – **WEIGHT:** 181 LBS
BORN: MARCH 30, 1986

- ⚽ WORLD CUP WINNER: 2010 SPAIN
- ⚽ EUROPEAN CHAMPION: 2012, 2018 SPAIN
- ⚽ CHAMPIONS LEAGUE WINNER: 13/14, 15/16, 16/17, 17/18 REAL MADRID
- ⚽ FIFA CLUB WORLD CUP WINNER: 2014, 2016, 2017, 2018 REAL MADRID

$ TRANSFERMARKT 2019 ESTIMATED VALUE:

28.5 MILLION

 @SergioRamos   **@SergioRamos**

When Googling the phrase, "How many times has Sergio Ramos . . ." chances are good that a top autofill option will be "been sent off." My teen consultant for this book, Jonah, said, "I think he's been sent off more times in El Clásico matches (the nickname for the match between rivals Real Madrid and FC Barcelona) than most players are in their entire careers." I checked: Five of Ramos's 25 career red cards have been during El Clásico, so Jonah may be onto something.

Ramos grew up in Seville watching the bull-fighting for which the city is famous. According to Ramos, "When I was young, I once had a dream career to be a bullfighter, but my mother was a little scared. After being advised by my older brother, Rene, I opted for football which is less dangerous."

Ramos began his career in the youth academy of his local club, Sevilla FC. He made more than 60 appearances between Sevilla B and the first team in his two years with the club, and on his website (SergioRamos.com) he writes fondly about his first game: "I had conquered my first great dream. The words of Joaquín Caparrós, who opted for a boy who had practically not played with lights in his life, I will never forget them: 'Kid, play as you know.' My thanks are eternal."

REAL MADRID TURNS RED

In the summer of 2005, a 19-year-old Ramos was transferred to Real Madrid for a transfer fee of €27 million. The fee set a record for most expensive Spanish defender ever, and it was the first purchase of a Spanish player by Real Madrid's president Florentino Perez. He told Ramos, "All I want is for you to be yourself," though one wonders whether he would have worded things differently had he known how many red cards Ramos would collect.

Ramos's 100th league appearance was in a game against his former club. "The match was even more emotional for me because it was against Sevilla," Ramos recalls. "It's always special to play against the club where I matured." Although Sevilla had an early lead, Madrid went on to win 3 to 2—a result that helped with the team's title race. It was, said Ramos, "Another one of those unforgettable nights in the Bernabéu [Real Madrid's home stadium]."

He began earning honors shortly after his Madrid debut. Real Madrid made both the FIFA and UEFA 2008 Teams of the Year, and Ramos finished 21st in nominations for European Player of the Year. In 2009, he became one of Real Madrid's four captains, and, on February 21, 2010, he had his 200th appearance for the club.

Upon joining Madrid, Ramos inherited the number 4 jersey of Madrid and Spain great, Fernando Hierro, and, on November 29, 2010, he tied Hierro's club record of 10 red card ejections—despite trailing him in appearances by 264 matches. When playing for Spain, however, Ramos wears the number 15 in honor of his close friend and team-mate Antonio Puerta, who passed away after he collapsed playing soccer in Sevilla's first La Liga match of the 2007–08 season. The two had talked about the number being lucky for them, and he wanted to carry on wearing it.

In addition to his ability to accumulate red cards, Ramos has been more proficient at scoring goals than is typical for defenders. To date, he has scored 59 goals in 419 appearances for the club, and five of those goals came in the 2006–07 season alone. The season before, he amassed four red cards, so per-haps the scales balanced out a bit.

Real Madrid beat arch-nemesis FC Barcelona to win the 2011 Copa del Ray (Spanish Championship). A possibly too-excited Ramos, standing on the team bus and waving to fans during celebrations after the tournament, accidently dropped the trophy under the bus and dented it. Yes, even professional athletes have clumsy moments.

Ramos's career with Madrid has been superlative. He has more than 650 appearances with the club and has been a part of their rich history of winning championships. Here are a few of his career highlights:

- In the 2014 UEFA Champions League Final, he headed in the tying stoppage time goal to send the game into extra time. Real Madrid went on to win 4 to 1 and captured "La Decima," their 10th European Cup.

- He won Player of the Match in the semifinal and final matches of the 2014 FIFA Club World Cup, scoring in both games and taking home the Golden Ball award for the tournament.

- In the 2016 UEFA Champions League Final, he scored twice—once in regular time, and once during penalty kicks. He was named Man of the Match for his efforts.

- He scored the critical tying goal in the 2016 UEFA Super Cup to ensure extra time. Real Madrid eventually won that game, and Ramos racked up another Man of the Match honor.

- His 2016–17 season was his highest-scoring to date, with a total of 10 goals. Real Madrid won La Liga and the European Cup that season along with their 33rd La Liga title—the first time they'd won both in a single season since 1957–58.

- The 2017–18 season brought Madrid and Ramos a third consecutive Champions League title. He was the first player to captain three trophy-winning tournaments in a row.

- Ramos and Barcelona legend Lionel Messi are the only players to have scored in each of the last 15 La Liga seasons.

- On February 6, 2019, Ramos played in his 40th El Clásico. A few days later, he became the seventh player in history to make more than 600 appearances for Real Madrid.

A STAR FOR SPAIN

Even after all those club triumphs, Ramos still had contributions to make for his country. He was an overnight sensation for Spain's U19 team, starting in four of the five matches on the road to their championship, the second in team history. He moved up to the Senior Spanish team just shy of his nineteenth birthday, which made him the youngest

Spanish player on the senior team in 55 years (unfortunately for Ramos, he didn't even get to hold that record for a year; Cesc Fàbregas broke it 340 days later).

By all accounts, Ramos's time with Spain has been a grand era for the nation in soccer. Here are just a few of his highlights with the Spanish Men's National Team:

- He scored his first two international goals in a single game—a 2006 FIFA World Cup qualifier against San Marino.

- In Spain's first ever World Cup Final Championship in 2010, Ramos played every minute of the tournament for Spain, helping the team not only win but also maintain shutouts in the knockout rounds against Portugal, Paraguay, Germany, and the Netherlands.

- He and Spain picked up more hardware (an amusing term for trophies) at the Euro 2012 tournament, scoring his tie-breaker penalty kick in the semifinals to beat Portugal. The team then celebrated their 4 to 0 trouncing of Italy in the final while Ramos wore a shirt honoring his late friend, Antonio Puerta.

- The 2018 World Cup was Ramos's fourth appearance in the tournament.

Ramos will likely be remembered for bringing excitement to both ends of the field—as a defender protecting his team's goal, and as a goal scorer at the opposite end of the pitch. His aggressive play may earn him a record-setting number of red cards, but certainly for his fans he more than makes up for it with solid defense and goal-scoring thrills.

FUN FACTS

⚽ Ramos earned his 100th international cap in a March 2013 World Cup qualifier versus Finland. With his usual flair, he scored in the match and became the youngest European to reach the 100-cap mark, edging out Lucas Podolski by 22 days.

⚽ Ramos's agent is his older brother, Rene Ramos.

⚽ He's a pretty good guitar player and quite romantic; he once played guitar on Spanish TV for his girlfriend at the time.

Spotlight
THE PITCH

The field on which soccer is played is often called "the pitch," which is a reference to cricket field terminology and the act of planting flags to mark the field.

An adult regulation field (the size on which all professionals play) is 100 to 130 yards long by 50 to 100 yards wide. Uniform lines less than 5 inches wide are drawn to mark the field; these are the painted white lines you typically see on grassy fields. The "goal lines" mark the shorter ends of the field where the goals are. The long sides of the field are called the "touch lines" because a ball leaving the field along one of these lines is going "into touch" (i.e., out of bounds), where field players can touch it with their hands to throw it back into play. All lines on the pitch are part of the area they bound, so a ball isn't into touch until it is completely past the line.

Regulation soccer goals are eight yards wide and eight feet tall. The rectangular box on the field in front of each goal is called the "goal box," which is marked six yards from the goal post. Then there is the larger "penalty area," which is marked 18 yards from each goal and includes the goal box. A "penalty mark" (often called "the spot") is

12 yards from the center of the goal, and a "penalty arc" is the semi-circle drawn 10 yards from the kick taker that all players have to stay outside of until the kick is taken. Each of the four corners has an arc drawn with a radius of less than one yard from the corner itself, indicating where the ball must be placed for corner kicks. A "halfway line" marks the center of the field parallel to the two goal lines, and a center circle radiates 10 yards from the center mark.

Although you won't see this on any pitch, my favorite referee instructor, Austin Gomez, taught his students to imagine an ice cream cone where the scoop is the center circle and the cone is a triangle drawn to the top of the penalty arc. Since this is where many plays occur, he said, it's best (as a referee) to stay out of the players' way when you're in the ice cream cone. Next time you're watching a game, try to imagine the ice cream cone and see how much of the action is taking place there.

Proper fields have natural grass, although some climates require artificially engineered playing surfaces (most players prefer natural grass). The science of growing perfect soccer grass has become an art form at the professional levels, where grass is specifically bred and cut to create a perfectly smooth playing surface.

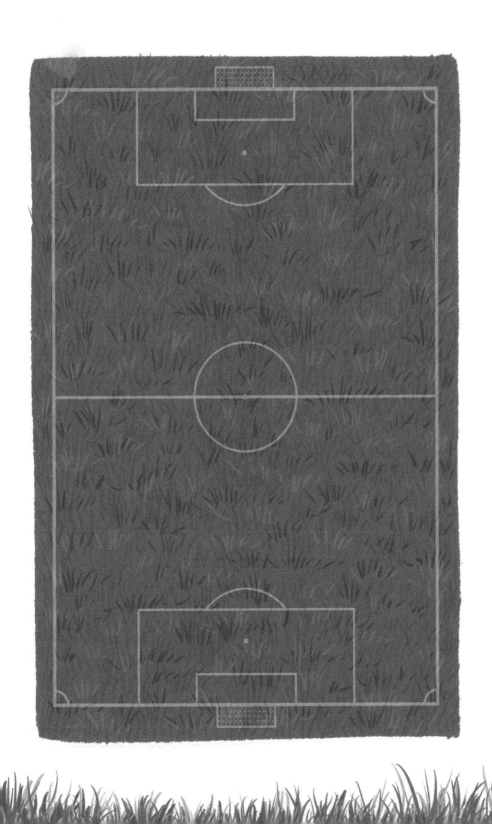

Legendary Great

JOHAN CRUYFF

I've often tried to imagine what it must have been like to watch the 1974 World Cup and see the very first "Cruyff Turn" before it even had a name. Dutch number 14 is just outside the penalty area, marked up tight. He fakes right, plants his left foot, drags the ball behind and left with his right foot, and takes off past the dumbfounded defender—and the Cruyff Turn is born.

My kids are still working on this move today, and that's just one of Johan Cruyff's legacies.

Cruyff was a legendary club player for Amsterdam's AFC Ajax (pronounced EYE-axe) from 1964 to 1973 (where he scored 190 goals in 240 caps) and Barcelona from 1973 to 1978 (with 48 goals in 143 caps). He also scored 33 goals in his 48 caps for the Netherlands, but his influence reached far beyond his inspirational play for both club and country.

His coaching and philosophy created the now-legendary FC Barcelona, and he reached players across the world with his "total football" approach to the game. As former player, Gary Lineker, tweeted upon Cruyff's passing, "Football has lost a man who did more to make the game beautiful than anyone else."

"Playing football is very simple, but playing simple football is the hardest thing there is," Cruyff said.

LIVERPOOL F.C.,
PREMIER LEAGUE

★ VIRGIL VAN DIJK ★

Virgil
VAN DIJK

4

POSITION: CENTER BACK
CLUB TEAM: LIVERPOOL F.C., PREMIER LEAGUE
NATIONAL TEAM: NETHERLANDS
HEIGHT: 6'4" – **WEIGHT:** 203 LBS
BORN: JULY 8, 1991

- ⚽ UEFA SUPER CUP 2019 LIVERPOOL FC
- ⚽ PLAYER OF THE YEAR: 18/19 LIVERPOOL AND PREMIERE LEAGUE
- ⚽ WINNER CHAMPIONS LEAGUE: 18/19 LIVERPOOL
- ⚽ SCOTTISH CHAMPION: 13/14, 14/15, 15/16 CELTIC FC

TRANSFERMARKT 2019 ESTIMATED VALUE:

$ 90 MILLION

 @VirgilvDijk   @VirgilvanDijk

Perhaps nowhere has the phrase, "rags to riches," been more appropriate than in Virgil van Dijk's story—as long as we're talking *dish* rags. This soccer superstar once washed dishes to get by as he worked his way through the developmental leagues. Jacques Lips, van Dijk's former boss at Oncle Jean Restaurant in Breda, Netherlands, said, "He was a good worker. He would scrub hard and do his job properly."

Luckily for soccer fans, van Dijk brought that same work ethic to the beautiful game.

Van Dijk was born to a Dutch father and Surinamese mother in the Netherlands. He was raised primarily by his mother after his father left the family; his father's absence from his life eventually led the young player to use only his first name on the back of his jersey. He was told repeatedly that he didn't have what it took to be a professional soccer player, and not just by his restaurant coworkers, who figured he could make a better living if he stayed with them. As a teenager, after a six-inch growth spurt in one year caused knee and groin issues, his coaches at the Willem II club in the Eredivisie league (the Netherlands' top professional soccer division) decided he had too many challenges to go pro. With that, he was free transferred to FC Gronigen.

Early in his time there, van Dijk almost died due to complications from appendicitis. His condition became so dire he even signed a will on his hospital bed.

But if that were the end of his story, he wouldn't be in this book.

SETTING RECORDS FOR CELTIC

Van Dijk made a full recovery, and once he was back to full strength, he outgrew Groningen. The club offered him to other teams around the Eredivisie, including the perennial powerhouse club AFC Ajax. Instead of staying close to home, however, he decided to move to Glasgow in 2013, where he joined the Scottish Premiership's legendary Celtic FC.

In his first year at Celtic, he was named to the Professional Footballers' Association (PFA) Scotland Team of the Year and was nominated to be the league's player of the year (he lost the title to his teammate, Kris Commons). He was also shortlisted for PFA Scotland's Players' 2015 Player Award, but he lost again to another teammate, Stefan Johansen.

His stint as a defender was a record-setting period for the Celtic. With van Dijk on the squad, Celtic went a whopping 1,256 minutes without allowing a single goal. That streak ended in a game against

Aberdeen, during which van Dijk got ejected when he, as the last line of defense before the keeper, took down an attacker. Playing without van Dijk proved to be too much for Celtic, and they lost both their shutout streak and 26-game winning streak.

Celtic won the Scottish League Championship and the League Cup during the 2014–15 season, but lost in the UEFA Europa League final, thus just missing their treble (winning three trophies in a single season). Van Dijk was named to the Team of the Season, but with Celtic failing to qualify for the 2015–16 UEFA Champions League, he began to look elsewhere for opportunities.

He transferred to Southampton F.C. in the English Premier League (EPL) in September 2015 for £13 million. He had a spectacular start, scoring his first goal for the Saints (as the team is called) in his third appearance, and the club signed him to a six-year contract eight months later.

On January 22, 2017, however, van Dijk's career took an unfortunate turn. While captaining the match versus Leicester (pronounced LESS-ter) City, he injured his ankle. Without him in the EPL Cup Final, Southampton went down 3 to 2 to Manchester United. The injury kept him out of the game for eight months.

As soon as the transfer window opened on January 1, 2018, van Dijk was sold to Liverpool F.C.

for £75 million; the club had been interested in him for roughly six months, causing Southampton to threaten legal action for pursuing a player outside the transfer window. The reported fee was a world record for a defender. In a BBC interview, van Dijk said he hoped to be remembered "as a legend of Liverpool." On April 28, 2019, he finally captured the honor of PFA Player of the Year, which ought to go a long way toward accomplishing that goal.

SURINAME OR NETHERLANDS?

With parents from two different countries, van Dijk could have chosen to play international soccer for either Suriname or the Netherlands. He opted for the latter and got his first cap playing for the Netherlands on October 10, 2015, in a UEFA Euro 2016 qualifier. He had fewer than 30 appearances by the summer of 2019, but was still awarded the title of captain in March 2018. Unfortunately for van Dijk, however, the Netherlands didn't qualify for the 2018 World Cup in Russia.

In a BBC interview, van Dijk talked about playing as a kid on the "obviously fantastic" Cruyff Courts—the soccer fields built all over the Netherlands (and around the world) by Johan Cruyff. "It was great," he said. "In the afternoon [on Sundays] you'd play five a side games, sometimes with seven or eight teams. If you lost you have to go out, if you won you stayed on. It was tough, hard work. But it was much better than it is right now, I think, because I don't see a lot of kids playing on the streets anymore, and I think that's a bit sad to see."

FUN FACTS

⚽ Van Dijk is a huge Disneyland fan. He loves how happy it is and watching his kids interact with the characters. He also likes Disney movies like *Aladdin* and *The Lion King*.

⚽ He is an avid fan of *Game of Thrones*, enjoying the thrills and plot twists.

⚽ He offers the following advice, which is clearly based on his personal experiences both on and off the pitch: "Believe in yourself. Never give up. Always work hard. Stay full of confidence."

Spotlight
SOCCER LEAGUES AND NATIONAL TEAMS

The world of soccer can be sprawling and complicated, but in the simplest terms, soccer is broken into two main groups: club and country.

REGIONS

While you may hear soccer fans talk about whether they prefer to watch "club vs. country," there are some things that are the same throughout soccer. Both club and country (aka national) teams are divided into regions around the globe. The six regions that *both* club leagues and national teams are split into are:

CONCACAF: Confederation of North, Central American, and Caribbean Association Football

AFC: Asian Football Confederation

CAF: Confederation of African Football

CONMEBOL: Confederación Sudamericana de Fútbol (the abbreviation uses the middle of the second word and the end of the last)

OFC: Oceania Football Confederation

UEFA: Union of European
Football Associations

In every region and virtually every country, there are soccer leagues and/or teams. UEFA's leagues are among the best-known worldwide, but they're by no means the only ones. CONCACAF, for example, has Major League Soccer (MLS) and Mexico's Liga MX. The AFC has leagues like the J1 in Japan and the Chinese Super League, but it also geographically includes leagues like the Afghan Premier League and Yemeni League. CAF has a long list of leagues throughout Africa (with a dozen or more clubs per league). CONMEBOL covers the Brazilian Campeonato and Argentine Primera Division (the famed clubs River Plate and Boca Juniors are in the latter). OFC has its own Champions League called the O-League where teams like Waitakere United (New Zealand), Hekari United (Papau New Guinea), and Wollongong Wolves (Australia) all play.

The bottom line is this: It's a big world, and almost everywhere you go, there's a soccer league.

CLUB

Club teams play in the hundreds of leagues worldwide. They range from youth soccer to amateur to professional teams, but their structures and organization vary widely around the world. Clubs play in both league games—like MLS in the United States or the EPL in England—and tournament games—such as UEFA Champions League.

Most leagues have different levels, and some allow teams to move up and down between those levels through promotion and relegation. This means, for instance, that the bottom teams in the best division can be relegated to the next division down, while the top teams in that lower division may get promoted to an upper division; it all depends on where each team is ranked on the table at the end of the season. The table rankings are based on points accumulated in league games: three points for a win, one point for a tie. Tie-breakers vary by league. With so much at stake, promotion and relegation sometimes make the so-called "race at the bottom of the table" as exciting as the fight for a league title.

In the United States, we have three different levels of leagues but no promotion and relegation between them. The MLS is the country's first (top) league. Below the MLS, the leagues have changed several times. Currently, the United Soccer League (USL) Championship (USLC) is the second division, and the USL League One (USL1)/National Independent Soccer Association (NISA) is the third division.

COUNTRY

Country refers to the national teams of each individual nation that are organized by the Fédération Internationale de Football Association (FIFA) into the same regional groups outlined above. National teams play in tournaments like the FIFA World Cup and the Olympics, and players are eligible to be selected to a certain country's team based on where they *or* their parents were born. Once a player has taken the field for their country, they can't switch to another national team (a marked difference from club soccer, where your favorite player can—and often does—get traded away from your favorite team). Appearances for a national team player are called "caps," and when a player makes their first appearance for their national team, they are called "capped" or "cap tied" because they can no longer switch nationalities.

National team games have different levels of importance. Games that don't count for tournaments are called "friendlies," even if the teams playing are bitter rivals. From the players' and coaches' standpoints, these games are typically for practice, staying fit, and trying out fresh players or formations; from the fan standpoint, they're often unpredictable and can be quite entertaining. Friendly matches aren't dictated by the FIFA calendar. Official FIFA matches must be scheduled during specific periods when club teams usually take a break.

"Qualifiers," on the other hand, are often high-stakes games that determine whether a team makes it to the next round of pre-tournament qualification for major tournaments like the World Cup and Olympics.

★ JOSHUA KIMMICH ★

Joshua
KIMMICH

★ ★ ★

32

POSITION: RIGHT BACK
CLUB TEAM: BAYERN MUNICH, BUNDESLIGA
NATIONAL TEAM: GERMANY
HEIGHT: 5'9" – WEIGHT: 159 LBS
BORN: FEBRUARY 8, 1995

- GERMAN CHAMPIONSHIP 15/16, 16/17, 17/18, 18/19 BAYERN MUNICH
- GERMAN CUP WINNER 15/16, 18/19 BAYERN MUNICH
- DFL SUPER CUP WINNER 16/17, 17/18, 18/19 BAYERN MUNICH
- CONFEDERATIONS CUP WINNER 2017 GERMANY

TRANSFERMARKT 2019 ESTIMATED VALUE:

$

79.8 MILLION

 @JoshuaKimmich   **@jok_32**

First things first: Let's get the name right. If you're pronouncing "Joshua" with a hard J and an SH as in the word, "shoe," think again. Germans pronounce the J like a Y, and Joshua Kimmich says his own name more like YOZ-oo-ah. However you say his name, Kimmich has been a stellar player for all teams lucky enough to roster him.

Kimmich's story of getting to his current club, Bayern Munich—which he wrote for *The Players' Tribune*—begins ominously: "There was a loud noise of shattering glass." Fortunately for fans everywhere, the broken windows didn't cause his parents to forbid him from playing soccer. On the contrary, his dad found a couple of goals that a nearby club was getting rid of, and he used them to build a mini-stadium for the neighborhood kids.

This little stadium was critical for the local kids of Bösingen—a town too small to have many playing surfaces. When the land was later sold, they moved the little stadium to Kimmich's grandfather's house. All that practice paid off when his team played VfB Stuttgart, the youth team under the then Bundesliga 1 club, perhaps the best club in the region. Kimmich scored a hat trick (three goals in one game) and, at age eight, caught the Stuttgart coach's attention.

His parents were unwilling to commit to the hour-long drive to Stuttgart, but the club remained

interested over the next few years as Kimmich found his way around regional teams. Finally, when he was twelve, his parents agreed to the long commute. After two years, he was one of only 18 players accepted to Stuttgart's prestigious residency academy.

Kimmich played at the academy for four years, but he became frustrated that he wasn't getting playing time on the club's third-division team. One of his coaches moved to RB Leipzig, and Kimmich joined him—taking on the challenges of living in a new city and trying to get to know new teammates while also undergoing rehabilitation from a recent groin injury.

He was able to recuperate in time for Leipzig's game against his old club, Stuttgart, and he was proud to be on the winning side, demonstrating to his former team that he was good enough for the third division. Leipzig's U19 team, including Kimmich, won the European Championship and was promoted to the second division. "I was a professional footballer," he remembers thinking at that point. "I didn't think things could get much better." He was about to be proven wrong.

A DREAM JOB: BAYERN MUNICH

In 2014, his agent told him the Bundesliga giant, Bayern Munich, had taken an interest in him. He met with Pep Guardiola, the team's legendary coach who had risen to stardom at the helm of FC Barcelona. "All I knew about Pep was from what I had seen on TV," said Kimmich. "I was so nervous, but as he walked in, I felt it right away—that trust. And immediately I knew: I wanted to play for Bayern." He joined Bayern in January 2015 for reported €7 million, debuting with the club the following September.

Bayern valued Kimmich for his intelligence and flexibility on the field. He played as both a defender and a midfielder, inspiring headlines such as, "Is Bayern Munich Utility Man Joshua Kimmich the Most Versatile Player in World Football?"

"Each position brings with it different things," he said to *Bleacher Report*, "and you can still learn a lot . . . while you're still young. I think it helps to become a more complete player."

Kimmich helped Bayern win trophies in his first season with the club. He played the full 120 minutes of the 2016 DFB-Pokal Final, and he also played in the 2017 DFL-Supercup Final, defeating arch-rival Dortmund in both games. In 2018, Bayern won a treble (three trophies in one season). Kimmich's 100th league appearance came on February 9, 2019, in a 3 to 1 victory over Schalke. He played every minute of Bayern's 34 Bundesliga matches that season and was second in the league for assists with a total of 13.

CHALLENGING TIMES WITH GERMANY

On the international side, Kimmich made a handful of appearances on the U17 and U18 teams before he became a more central player on the U19 and U21 teams. He was part of the 2014 U19 squad that won the European U19 Championship, beating Portugal in the final 1 to 0. When Germany's provisional team for Euro 2016 was announced, Kimmich got his first call up to *"Die Mannschaft"* (which translates to "the team" in English—one of many phrases that sounds better in German), as the senior German team is known.

Germany reached the semifinals of Euro 2016 with Kimmich stable as the starting right back after getting his first cap in the last game of group stage play. He was ultimately named to the UEFA Team of the Tournament.

Kimmich scored his first international goal in September 2016 during World Cup qualification. Germany won all their qualifying games for the Russia World Cup and were on a high leading into the 2017 Confederations Cup. Kimmich started in all five matches, racked up two assists, and helped Germany lift its first Confederations Cup trophy.

Things may have looked great for Kimmich and the defending champions heading into the World

Cup in Russia in June 2018, but that didn't last. In the opening round, they lost to both Mexico and South Korea (South Korea scored twice in stoppage time—an absolute heartbreaker for Germany fans) but managed to squeak out a last-minute goal to beat Sweden in their only victory before being sent home. It was a disappointingly early exit for a team that had come in with such high hopes.

Germany's troubles, however, were not over.

The suffering continued as the team performed poorly at 2018 UEFA Nations League. They did not advance to the finals and, even worse, were relegated to League B for the following year. As Germany tries to rebuild, we can expect the team's long-time coach, Joachim Löw, to take advantage of Kimmich's versatility and leadership, particularly as he is now the team's captain.

Deutsche Welle's article assessing the German team's future offers this note on Kimmich:

"The way in which the 24-year-old reads the game is a quality Löw greatly admires, as he did with Lahm back in the day. Unlike the World Cup winning captain though, Kimmich is a vocal leader out on the pitch who is quicker to get his feathers get ruffled. It's that tenacity which makes him such a key component in an otherwise young and mild-mannered side."

FUN FACTS

⚽ Kimmich's parents initially refused an invitation for him to start training with Stuttgart's youth team until the coach personally visited their home and convinced them.

⚽ In February 2019, Kimmich tossed his jersey to a young fan with a sign asking Kimmich to wish him a happy birthday. Judging by the look on the kid's face, it was a very happy day.

⚽ His *spitzname* (German for nickname) is Josh or Jo, which in German sounds like YO!

Honorable Mentions
DEFENDERS

LEONARDO BONUCCI

Italian Leonardo Bonucci gets an honorable mention for a number of reasons, not least because he plays for Serie A's mighty Juventus—which is the team favored by Kyle Krause, the owner of my own beloved team, the Des Moines Menace. But really, Bonucci qualifies easily for this list simply based on his performance on the pitch.

Acquired by Turin's Juventus (pronounced yoo-VEN-toos) in July 2010, he was immediately added to the starting team and has had more than 250 appearances for the club. Bonucci and his teammates Andrea Barzagli and Georgio Chiellini earned the collective nickname "BBC," and became known as one of the toughest defensive lines in European soccer. Bonucci pointed out that their approach was holistic. "The defensive operation includes the forwards, as well," he said. "Our work is made easier by our forwards . . . [acting as] our first defenders. They use full-field pressing on the opposition back line, allowing us to be more aggressive." Such a system has proved formidable: Juventus won six Serie A titles in a row from 2012 to 2017.

Representing Italy, Bonucci played in the 2010 and 2014 World Cups, the 2012 and 2016 European Championships (Italy earned second place in 2012), and the 2013 FIFA Confederations Cup (where they took third place). Bonucci has won several player and team of the year honors.

In 2017, Bonucci spent a season playing for AC Milan. He was transferred back to Juventus the following season, but, while playing for Milan, he scored on stalwart Juventus keeper, Gianluigi Buffon—the goal that ended Buffon's staggering 959-minute Serie A clean sheet record.

Perhaps not surprisingly, Juventus fans were none too pleased with Bonucci, even when he returned to his familiar club. But when Internet trolls started saying awful things about his family, Bonucci retorted that he wanted to live and raise his children in a world without "violence in gestures, words, and thoughts."

HÉCTOR BELLERÍN

Spaniard Héctor Bellerín's Twitter feed is, currently, an adorable collection of rehab vlogs (he's been out with an ACL injury since January 2019), campy photos of fashion and soccer, and—most charming of all—visits with his fans. He spent time in the sensory room at Arsenal's home Emirates Stadium in London and shocked Arsenal supporters at a bar in Los Angeles.

He has declared Arsenal "home" after signing a deal with them in 2016 that goes through 2022. Known for his speed and dribbling, Bellerín blew up Arsenal's Twitter when he ran the 40-meter dash in 4.41 seconds, which was .23 seconds faster than the first 40 meters of Usain Bolt's world record. Arsenal won the FA Cup Final in 2015 and the Community Shield in 2015 and 2017.

Bellerín has also represented Spain numerous times on various youth teams and has made three appearances for the senior Spanish team since 2016.

MAYA YOSHIDA

Maya hails from Nagasaki, Japan, and has represented Japan's National Team since his promotion to the Olympic team in 2008. He has played for the Premier League club Southampton since 2012, making 146 appearances (to date), but he made history in Japan even before he started playing in the Premiership.

Yoshida came up as a midfielder through Nagoya Grampus's youth team but switched to center back defending upon joining their senior team in 2007. He scored the team's first-ever goal in the AFC Champions League (colloquially known as Asian Champions League) on March 10, 2009.

He made the jump to Europe in 2010 to join a Japanese teammate playing at VVV-Venlo in the Netherlands, and he went on to score the "Goal of the Season" off a bicycle kick against PSV Eindhoven on September 11, 2011. In August 2012, BBC headlines declared, "Southampton Sign Maya Yoshida, Japan's Olympic Captain." Yoshida was the first Asian player to achieve 100 Premier League appearances.

He made his national team debut in a 2011 AFC Asian Cup qualifier and subsequently helped Japan win the final in that tournament. He played in all of Japan's 2014 World Cup opening round games, as well as every minute of Japan's group stage games at the 2018 World Cup.

Legendary Great

ALEXI LALAS

I can hear the groans as I write this, but hear me out!

Today, American Alexi Lalas is known for his controversial opinions from the broadcast chair and over Twitter. But back in the day, he was part of the US Men's National Team that competed in the 1994 World Cup. Both on and off the pitch, he has had a huge role in pulling soccer out of the nerdy, specialized corners of the world and creating the space for American soccer supporter culture to thrive.

In the June 12, 1994, *New York Times* article, "WORLD CUP '94; Awake, America! Let Soccer Ring," Lalas encouraged Americans to accept the culture of the World Cup—no matter where it leads: "We need the culture police in the stands, saying 'Hey, it's culture, leave it alone. So what if they're sacrificing a goat, let it go. It's the World Cup."

I read that in 1994 and thought, "I'm going to spend my life traveling the world and learning about world cultures through soccer." Now that I've been to 10 World Cups and watched soccer games in 14 countries, I can honestly say I've never seen an in-stadium sacrifice—but I *have* seen parts of the world I never would have visited otherwise.

So, for better or worse, the outspoken, orange-haired, goatee-sporting, guitar-playing crazy man Alexi Lalas, is my choice for legendary great defender.

QD HUANGHAI,
CHINA LEAGUE ONE

★ YAYA TOURÉ ★

Yaya TOURÉ

24

POSITION: MIDFIELDER
CLUB TEAM: QD HUANGHAI, CHINA LEAGUE ONE
NATIONAL TEAM: IVORY COAST
HEIGHT: 6'2" – WEIGHT: 172 LBS
BORN: MAY 13, 1983

- ⚽ AFRICAN FOOTBALLER OF THE YEAR 2011, 12, 13, 14 IVORY COAST
- ⚽ FIFA CLUB WORLD CUP WINNER 2010 FC BARCELONA
- ⚽ AFRICA CUP WINNER 2015 IVORY COAST
- ⚽ UEFA SUPER CUP WINNER 09/10 FC BARCELONA

TRANSFERMARKT 2019 ESTIMATED VALUE:

$

285,000

 @yayatoure   @yayatoure

Yaya Touré is an excellent example of the global appeal of soccer. He represents both Africa, with more than 100 caps for the Ivory Coast, and Asia, since he plays club soccer with China League One's team, Qindao Huanghai. In addition to logging some miles in physical travel around the world, he has also traveled all over the field. He began his soccer career as an aspiring striker, which is a midfield position where the player covers almost the entire field, as opposed to an attacking or defensive midfielder.

He grew up in Bouake, a large city in central Ivory Coast, in a family that struggled to make ends meet. He and his older brother Kolo (who also became a soccer star) worked to supplement their dad's income by shining shoes. Touré loved playing soccer in the streets even if he usually ran barefoot. "Boots [what Europeans call soccer cleats] were very expensive," he told *The Guardian* in 2011, "and when there are seven in your family and you say you want to buy a pair, your father wants to kill you."

Touré acknowledged in that interview that, "Life was always a struggle when I was growing up, but that was before the [civil] war came. Now when you go back home you can see in people's faces that life is more difficult than before." He remains dedicated to his home country even while he plays soccer on the other side of the world, adding, "That is why it is important to keep going back. Whatever we can do to help, it's very important to show the people I'm still with them. They are amazing, they love football, and we have to do something for them."

Touré's devotion to Ivory Coast is tied to his championing of environmental causes. In 2013, he became a Goodwill Ambassador for the United Nations Environment Program (UNEP) to fight the poaching of African elephants for the illegal ivory trade.

"I became a UNEP Goodwill Ambassador to spread the message that poaching and other forms of wildlife crimes is not only a betrayal of our responsibility to safeguard threatened species," he said, "but a serious threat to the security, political stability, economy, natural resources, and cultural heritage of many countries."

ASEC Mimosas club in Ivory Coast's Ligue 1 gave Touré his start as a youth player, and he made his professional debut with them at age eighteen. His club career soon became something of a world tour; he played with Beveren (Belgium), Metalurh Donetsk (Ukraine), Olympiacos (Greece), and Monaco before landing at FC Barcelona (Spain) in 2007 for a rumored €10 million. He played more than 100 matches for Barcelona and took part in their epic 2009 calendar year, during which they won six trophies.

The year 2010 brought Touré the opportunity to join his brother and Ivory Coast teammate, Kolo Touré, in Manchester City for a reported £24 million transfer fee—which made him the Premiership's first £200,000-a-week player. He emphasized, however, that the transfer wasn't about money. "I saw a lot of things in the press about why I left Barcelona. But for me, I wanted to play with my brother, Kolo, one time. In football, you do not know what will happen tomorrow, and [to play with Kolo] was very important to me."

"I want to do something important with my brother," said the younger Touré in an interview with *The Telegraph*. "We will set up a big foundation to help young people. It is a great pleasure to bring something back." Touré's charity efforts have included work with Tackle Africa, a nonprofit organization that teaches HIV prevention and sexual health through soccer, and Soccer Aid, a UNICEF fundraiser that works to ensure all kids have access to play.

In his first season playing for Manchester City, Touré immediately improved things for the club. He scored the only goal in the 2011 FA Cup Final, bringing home the first major trophy Man City (as the club is known) had earned in 35 years. He was named the 2011 African Footballer of the Year, which is a big deal for a midfielder—the previous dozen awardees had been forwards. It was an even bigger deal (though perhaps not exactly a surprise anymore) when he won again in 2012, 2013, and 2014.

Touré continued to find success at Man City, repeatedly winning Man of the Match and getting promoted to one of the team's captains. He won 2013 BBC African Footballer of the Year and made the 2014 PFA Team of the Year roster. He became the only second midfielder to have 20 goals in a season, which helped Man City win its second Premier League title in three years.

Unfortunately, he also faced racism at other stadiums. Racism is still an issue in international soccer, despite the campaigning of groups like "Kick It Out" and "Say No to Racism" to end the ugliness. Touré continues to speak out against racism to this day.

"It was a tough time," Touré told Marca.com in 2019, "and the worst thing about it was I had to live through it every game." He encourages teammates to stick up for one another, saying, "If a footballer is offended, then the whole team should leave the pitch."

Over Touré's later years in England, there were on-and-off reports of conflict between Touré and Man City's coach Pep Guardiola. It's tough to distinguish rumor from fact, but in May 2018, the announcement came that that he would leave the team at the end of the season. After a few months at his former Greek Super League team, Olympiacos, he put an end to the rumors that he would retire by joining the China League One club, Qingdao Huanghai.

WITH YOUR COUNTRY, IT'S UNBELIEVABLE

Touré debuted on the Ivory Coast's national team in 2014 and quickly became a regular in the lineup. He was a part of their historic first World Cup in 2006, playing in all three matches. In 2010, he scored the first goal in Ivory Coast's winning match against North Korea. By 2014, he was team captain, led his team to their opening match win against Japan, and was named FIFA Man of the Match.

He has represented Ivory Coast six times in the Africa Cup of Nations, including their runner-up efforts in 2006 and 2012 and championship run in 2015. The 2015 championship was a marathon of a game that required 11 penalty kicks after overtime to determine a winner.

"When you win with your club, it's quite amazing," he said after winning the AFCON final. "With your country, it's unbelievable."

FUN FACTS

⚽ Touré got his first pair of "boots," or soccer shoes, at age ten.

⚽ In 2014, FIFA named him Man of the Match in Ivory Coast's opening game against Japan, which they won 2 to 1.

⚽ He's known to stay after practice and work on his free kicks. Practice makes perfect!

⚽ He has donated PUMA sporting goods to children in West Africa.

Spotlight
LAWS OF THE GAME

Every year, FIFA issues *Laws of the Game*, a roughly 150-page booklet outlining in great detail how soccer is played. In addition to studying this book, higher-level referees participate in rules meetings and weekly conference calls on officiating.

The laws are broken down into 17 sections:

1. The Field of Play
2. The Ball
3. The Players
4. The Players' Equipment
5. The Referee
6. The Other Match Officials
7. The Duration of the Match
8. The Start and Restart of Play
9. The Ball In and Out of Play
10. Determining the Outcome of a Match
11. Offside
12. Fouls and Misconduct
13. Free Kicks
14. The Penalty Kick
15. The Throw-In
16. The Goal Kick
17. The Corner Kick

Soccer seems very simple until you sit down and read the entire rule book!

Without studying the whole thing, however, there are a few rules that are helpful for spectators to understand.

- ⚽ Full-side soccer is played 11 vs. 11 players who play for 45 minutes, have a half time break of usually 15 minutes, then play another 45 minutes attacking the opposite goal. This gives each team equal opportunity to have "the wind at their backs," as it were. (Sometimes that's a metaphor. Sometimes that's literal.)

- ⚽ Balls that go over the end lines on either side of the goal are put back into play by kicks. It's a goal kick if an attacker last touched it and a corner kick if a defender did.

- ⚽ "Playing the ball out on the sides" means the opposite team from the one that last touched it throws it back into play.

- ⚽ If a player breaks the rules, the referee can penalize them by giving a free kick to the opposite team and possibly a yellow (caution) or red (ejection) card.

- ⚽ A second yellow card for the same player in a match will result in ejection.

Of all the details in *Laws of the Game*, Law 11: Offside is considered the most confusing. It boils down to this: Without the offside (not "offsides"—it's not plural) rule, forwards might just hunker down by the opposing goal for the entire game, waiting for a teammate to shoot a long pass their way for an easy scoring opportunity. Since that would be boring to watch, the offside rule says that a player must always have at least two opponents (one of which can be, and usually is, the keeper) or the ball between them and the goal they're attacking. As long as you do that, you don't have to worry about the rest of the offside rule.

Spotlight
THE WORLD CUP

There's no sporting event in the world bigger than the World Cup. The World Series and the Super Bowl both pale in comparison. It is more important in the soccer world than even the Olympics, and while the Olympics are hosted in one city, the World Cup takes place across an entire country, or sometimes across multiple countries. Typically, there are 10 to 12 stadiums that host matches for the month-long World Cup Finals tournament.

The World Cup is played every four years, and it is hosted on a different continent, generally on a rotating basis. FIFA representatives meet and vote on bids submitted by potential host countries. Russia hosted in 2018, Qatar will host in 2022, and 2026 will be hosted by the United Bid of the United States, Mexico, and Canada.

The road to these Finals is paved by qualifiers. Within the FIFA regions (see Spotlight: Soccer Leagues and National Teams on page 37), nations compete for up to three years before the World Cup to become representative nations from their region. Qualifying for the CONCACAF region (which includes the United States) was three years for the 2018 tournament, but it was cut to just under two years for the 2022 tournament. The regions and their 2018 World Cup allotments are:

CONCACAF: Received 3.5 slots to the World Cup Finals for the 35 teams that started qualifying. Our .5 is a playoff with AFC. Our region sent three teams to Russia.

AFC: 4.5 slots for 46 teams. Five teams sent to Russia.

CAF: 5 slots for 54 teams.

CONMEBOL: 4.5 slots for 10 teams. Five teams sent to Russia.

OFC: .5 slots for 11 teams. OFC's .5 is a playoff with CONMEBOL. Zero teams qualified for Russia.

UEFA: 13 (+1 for Russia hosting) for 54+1 teams. 14 teams sent to the World Cup Finals.

During the December before the World Cup (usually about six months before the tournament), FIFA hosts the World Cup Draw. This schedule may be altered for the 2022 World Cup, which will be held in November and December instead of the traditional June and July schedule to accommodate for Qatar's weather. The World Cup Draw divides the qualified teams into groups.

The first two weeks of the tournament are called the "group stage," during which teams play each other in a round-robin format (each team plays the three other teams in their group once). Teams get three points for a win, one point for a tie, and no points for a loss. There are usually three games played every day in the first round, but the last of the three games are played simultaneously so no one will know how the group table will end up until both games end.

This has been important several times in my personal experience, my favorite being at the Korea World Cup. In 2002, the United States was playing Poland in the final game of the group stage while the host, Korea, played Portugal in a different city. We had been enjoying a fantastic tournament so far. The United States was a fresh young team that was exciting to watch. We had beaten Portugal, who had some of the best-ranked players in the world on their squad (like Figo, a FIFA-ranked top 5 player) by a score of 3 to 2 (and one of their goals had been an own goal by our own Jeff Agoos; we spent those two weeks singing, "Agoos has more goals than Figo!" in a little self-deprecating fun). Then, we managed to hold onto a tie with Korea in a stadium that was, by far, the loudest place I've ever experienced in my life.

Our game with Poland did not get off to a good start, and it only got worse as it progressed. It was a lesson in not taking anything for granted: The United States had played so well against the supposed best team in the group, but Poland scored in the third and fifth minutes, leaving us eliminated as things stood. Around the 70th minute, we noticed loud cheers from the Korean section around the corner from us. None of us had Internet access on our phones, so we were wildly gesturing to the Koreans trying to figure out what was going on. A victory for Korea was the only way we were going to advance out of the group if we lost to Poland. They were jumping and smiling and holding up two fingers. We were desperately trying to figure out what that meant when an even louder jubilant shout rang out from the Korean section. We finally learned that the two fingers were for two red card ejections against Portugal. Then, Korea scored to win their match 1 to 0, which meant we would advance despite our loss. That night celebrating our advancement and the host team's advancement was probably the most fun I've ever had at a World Cup.

OUT OF THE FRYING PAN, INTO THE FIRE

As wild as the first round can be, it only heats up as the tournament moves on to the knock-out stages, so named because there must be a winner and a loser in every game. Points are tallied at the end of the round robin, and the remaining bracket for the tournament is filled in with first-place round-robin teams playing their second-place counterparts.

Since games can no longer end in a tie, the knock-out round adds two 15-minute periods of extra time that are not "sudden-death"—all 30 minutes are played. If the score is still tied, the game is decided by a penalty kick shoot-out, where teams take turns taking penalty kicks at one end of the field for five rounds. If no winner is decided in five rounds, the kicks are then one for one until one team misses and the other scores to determine the winner. It's pretty much the most stressful way to get eliminated from the World Cup.

There have been two World Cup trophies: the first was originally named "Victory," but changed in 1946 to the Jules Rimet Trophy to honor the FIFA president by the same name. It was awarded from 1930 to 1970, when Brazil won the World Cup for the third time and was allowed to keep the Jules Rimet Trophy forever, per his instructions given in 1930.

There's some adventurous folklore surrounding the Jules Rimet Trophy. It was in the possession of the 1938 champion, Italy, during World War II, when the Italian vice president of FIFA secretly hid the trophy in a shoe box under his bed to prevent the Nazis from stealing it. Four months before the 1966 World Cup, the trophy was stolen from an exhibit at Westminster Central Hall, but luckily was found in a South London suburban garden by a dog named Pickles. The trophy was stolen again in 1983 from its display at Brazilian Football Confederation headquarters. It has never been recovered.

The new trophy was chosen out of 53 submissions across seven countries to FIFA's call for ideas. The winning sculpture by Italian Silvio Gazzaniga is made of 11 pounds of 18-karat gold with two rings of green malachite stone in the base. Although Germany has won the new trophy three times, new rules state this trophy cannot be won outright, but each winner receives a bronze replica to keep.

★ N'GOLO KANTÉ ★

N'Golo
KANTÉ

7

POSITION: DEFENSIVE MIDFIELDER
CLUB TEAM: CHELSEA, PREMIER LEAGUE
NATIONAL TEAM: FRANCE
HEIGHT: 5'6" – WEIGHT: 159 LBS
BORN: MARCH 29, 1991

⚽ PLAYER OF THE YEAR 16/17
   CHELSEA FC, PREMIER LEAGUE
⚽ FOOTBALLER OF THE YEAR 2017 FRANCE
⚽ WORLD CUP WINNER 2018 FRANCE
⚽ ENGLISH CHAMPION 2016 LEICESTER
   CITY, 2017 CHELSEA FC

TRANSFERMARKT 2019 ESTIMATED VALUE:

$

114 MILLION

 @nglkante   @nglkante

I t might be clear enough from the *90min* head-line, "N'Golo Kanté: How Chelsea Hit the Jackpot When They Signed the Diminutive Frenchman," that Kanté is very good at what he does. In case you're still wondering, though, the article also pointed out, "When a central defensive midfielder can finish 11th in the Ballon d'Or (awarded by FIFA to the best international player), you know he's the real deal."

Kanté's parents immigrated from Mali to Paris in 1980, and Kanté was born in Paris in 1991. They lived in a small apartment in the Parisian suburbs. As a child, Kanté would pick up trash for profit on the streets of Paris, trying to find a little extra cash for his family. When the World Cup came to France in 1998, a young Kanté saw a team of immigrants playing for France win the World Cup, and this inspired him.

His sister was playing soccer in the youth system at the nearby Suresnes club, and although no one quite remembers when N'Golo started tagging along with her to practice, he started playing with the club as well sometime after the 1998 World Cup, riding a push scooter to practice.

Suresnes had had star players "poached" by bigger teams from them in the past, but every-one missed the short, unassuming Kanté. "It was because he was a little guy, not spectacular," mused

Suresnes's deputy manager later. "He did not play for himself, he played for the team."

Photos of Kanté on his youth teams show him at only the shoulder height of most of his teammates, but his selfless playing style proved valuable in his decade with Suresnes and beyond. He joined the reserve team of Boulogne (in France's second division) through a Suresnes, connection and made his professional debut in Ligue 2 on the last game of the season in May 2012. He played in every league game save one in the following season, when Boulogne had been relegated to the third tier of French soccer.

In 2013, Kanté had the opportunity to play in all 38 games for Stade Malherbe Caen back up in Ligue 2. They finished the season in third place, earning a promotion to Ligue 1—France's top league. He continued to represent the team in every 2014 match (except one, which he had to sit out on a red card). According to the BBC, he recovered the ball more times that season than any other player in Europe.

His quiet, consistent performance got noticed, and in August 2015, he joined Leicester (pronounced LESS-ter) City on a four-year contract reported at €8 million (£5.6 million). During the preseason, BBC's lead soccer writer, Phil McNulty, predicted that Leicester would finish second from the bottom—a position that would have meant relegation. Instead, they won the league.

Kanté was a huge part of that accomplishment. He had 175 tackles for the season and led in interceptions at 157. Leicester's goalkeeper, Mark Schwarzer, called Kanté's performance, "Second to none—his positional sense was incredible. He was so incredibly quiet but read the game so well. It was like you were being ambushed." Kanté was further honored for his efforts when he was rostered on the PFA Team of the Year for 2015–16.

Less than a year after joining Leicester, however, Kanté was signed away by Chelsea for a reported £32 million. "I am so happy to have signed for one of the biggest clubs in Europe," he said. "It is a dream come true for me. The opportunity to work with Antonio Conte, a brilliant coach, and some of the best players in the world was simply too good to turn down. My first season in English football was very special and now I hope to go on to achieve even more during my time as a Chelsea player. I am looking forward to meeting up with my new teammates and helping the club achieve a lot of success."

Kanté has been described as grateful and humble, and although he was certainly pleased by his lucrative contract with Chelsea, he didn't let it go to his head. When Chelsea allegedly offered to pay him via an offshore account to avoid taxes, he had his lawyer politely decline, saying, "He simply wants a normal salary."

INTEREST FROM MALI, PATIENCE FOR FRANCE

His time with Chelsea has been outstanding by any measure. The French sports newspaper *L'Équipe* named him the sixth best player in the world in 2016, and that same year he won his second consecutive PFA Team of the Year spot (among other awards). He became the first player since 1993 to win back-to-back top-flight (first division) English titles with two different clubs. And, of course, there was that Ballon d'Or nomination.

And we haven't even discussed his participation with a national team yet.

Since he was born to Malian parents, the Malian national team approached Kanté in the hopes he would play for them in the 2015 Africa Cup of Nations. He declined. They came back in January 2016, and Kanté turned them down again. He wanted to play for France, the country in which he was born, and he knew that if he played even once for Mali, the opportunity to play for France would be gone. So, he waited. He had not even been called up to the French youth teams by this point, but he waited.

Finally, in March 2016, Kanté got what he had been waiting for. He was called up to play for France in a couple friendlies against the Netherlands and Russia. He played the second half of the

Netherlands match and, on his twenty-fifth birthday, started against Russia *and* scored the opening goal. His first official match for France came on June 10, 2016, in the opening game of the Euro 2016 tournament. France made it to the final, and although they lost to Portugal after extra time, Kanté's value to the team was clear.

There's a sort of beautiful poetry to Kanté's first World Cup in 2018. Two decades after he watched his home country host the prestigious event and win the title with a team made up largely of immigrants like himself, he, too, had the opportunity to represent his country in that same tournament. He played in all seven games, the last being the Final, relentlessly pick-pocketing the best players in the world with little apparent effort.

After the tournament, his teammates talked about how inspirational Kanté had been, encouraging them to remember and emulate the 1998 champions. They made up a song for him that honored his efforts in the game against Argentina. True to form, though, when the team celebrated its win and everyone was joyously posing for photographs with the trophy, Kanté had to be prompted by teammates to follow suit. He preferred to hang back and watch his teammates celebrate, as selfless in victory as he is in his play.

FUN FACTS

⚽ When Kanté joined Leicester, he had to be convinced not to run to practice. He finally bought a used Mini Cooper when they persuaded him that it wasn't proper for a Premiership player to run to practice.

⚽ He was in a minor fender bender in that same Mini Cooper on his way to Chelsea's League Cup tie versus Arsenal. He played the full 90 minutes, and still showed up to practice two days later with the side mirror taped to the dinged car.

⚽ He once went to a local mosque in London's King's Cross neighborhood after missing his train, where he met an Arsenal fan who invited him to his house, in keeping with the Islamic teaching to welcome people for dinner. Kanté accepted, beat everyone at the FIFA video game, then watched *Match of the Day* with them. Chelsea confirmed the story, saying, "That's typical N'Golo."

Spotlight
WOMEN IN SOCCER

Staggering improvements have been made in women's soccer over the past 20 years, certainly in the United States, but perhaps even more so elsewhere around the world.

When the United States hosted the Women's World Cup in 1999, there were very few other countries that invested in their women's teams. Today, we are still a long way from equality in soccer, but there are more leagues developing, and the quality of international women's soccer has skyrocketed.

After several attempts at a women's professional league in the United States, we are finally seeing the current National Women's Soccer League (NWSL) have some success. Following the 2019 Women's World Cup, there were NWSL games that garnered bigger crowds than some MLS games, and ESPN has started televising women's games more consistently.

By far, the United States has the most historically successful women's squad in the world. They captured their fourth star (teams earn a star for every championship) at the 2019 Women's World Cup Finals in Lyon, France, having won the previous stars in 1991, 1999, and 2015. They also finished second in

2011 and third in 1995, 2003, and 2007. In Olympic soccer, they hold four gold medals and a silver medal.

Despite these incredible successes, however, the women playing soccer today still fight for pay and investment equity with their male counterparts. The US Soccer motto is "One Nation, One Team," and that "one team" appears to mainly refer to the US Men's National Team. Players on the US Women's National Team are currently paid roughly 77 percent of what the men are paid, and investments in the development of women's soccer lag behind similar investments made in the men's game.

Fans around the country have made their support for these women plain, inspired by both their play and their fight for equality.

★ CHRISTIAN PULISIC ★

Christian ★ ★ ★
PULISIC

22

POSITION: MIDFIELDER
CLUB TEAM: CHELSEA, PREMIER LEAGUE
NATIONAL TEAM: UNITED STATES
HEIGHT: 5'8" – WEIGHT: 139 LBS
BORN: SEPTEMBER 18, 1998

⚽ PLAYER OF THE YEAR 2017 UNITED STATES
⚽ GERMAN CUP WINNER 16/17
   BORUSSIA DORTMUND
⚽ GERMAN U19 BUNDESLIGA CHAMPION
   15/16 BORUSSIA DORTMUND U19
⚽ GERMAN U17 BUNDESLIGA CHAMPION
   14/15 BORUSSIA DORTMUND U17

TRANSFERMARKT 2019 ESTIMATED VALUE:

$

60 MILLION

 @cpulisic_10   **@cmpulisic**

When Christian Pulisic sat down on the pitch after the United States had failed to qualify for the 2018 World Cup, he perfectly expressed the shattered dreams of millions of American soccer fans. The good news is that Pulisic's drive and passion for the game can help those same fans feel a little more optimistic about the future.

Pulisic is the son of George Mason University soccer players, Kelley and Mark Pulisic (Mark also played pro indoor soccer and spent time coaching). His parents knew the formula for creating great soccer players around the world: playing futsal (an indoor soccer-like game that emphasizes ball skills) and street soccer early on instead of going to an organized practice. His dad created Detroit's first futsal league.

Born in 1998, he is among the first generation of American kids with access to international soccer games televised on a regular basis. In 2005, at age seven, Pulisic spent a year in England, where he was immersed in soccer culture while his mom was a Fulbright scholar.

That year in England, he played for Brackley Town's youth program, an experience that, he said, "Really brought on my passion for the game. I just started to love it so much and I said, 'Wow, I'm pretty good! I think I can do something with this game.'"

Meanwhile, his parents' philosophy of free play combined with the opportunities to kick a ball around with local kids (or skilled family members, such as his mom and dad) turned out to be an ideal combination to allow Pulisic to develop to his full potential. His father would later say, "We didn't so much *develop* Christian as we just didn't *ruin* him."

When they returned to the United States, Pulisic spent a year in Michigan before returning to the Hershey, Pennsylvania, area where he was born. There, he joined the US Soccer Development Academy through PA Classics from 2008 to 2015. His family would take trips to Europe in the summers, where he could experience the playing programs of international clubs.

He was playing with kids two age groups above him but could run circles around most of the other players on the field. Teams in Europe began expressing interest in him, but he waited until 2015 to join the German Bundesliga's Borussia Dortmund at age seventeen. He chose them because of their reputation for developing young players, something Pulisic still believes is sorely lacking in the MLS.

Pulisic went on a streak with Dortmund's youth team with 10 goals and 8 assists in just 15 games, and by winter break, he was promoted to the senior team. He was a record-breaking phenomenon almost immediately. Here are just a few of his notable accomplishments:

- ⚽ 1/30/16 Youngest player in 2015–16 Bundesliga season

- ⚽ 2/18/16 Youngest American to play in a UEFA match

- ⚽ 3/29/16 Youngest American to play in a World Cup Qualifier

- ⚽ 4/17/16 Youngest foreign player to score in Bundesliga (fourth youngest overall)

- ⚽ 4/23/16 Youngest player to score twice in Bundesliga

- ⚽ 5/28/16 Youngest player to score for US Men's National Team (USMNT) in the modern era

- ⚽ 9/2/16 Youngest American to score a brace (two goals in one game) in the USMNT's 6 to 0 smash of World Cup Qualifying hopefuls St. Vincent and the Grenadines

- ⚽ 5/27/17 Youngest American to win a major European trophy

Moving to Germany as a teenager, however, was not easy. Americans aren't allowed to play in Europe until they turn eighteen, but the seventeen-year-old Pulisic was able to get dual citizenship in Croatia through his grandfather, allowing him to start playing with the team he had already been practicing with. He was still in school, too, only now all his classes were in German. Later, he'd impress fans and journalists alike with postseason interviews given entirely in excellent German, but early on his mother said he didn't always know if the class he was sitting in was math or science. Practice makes perfect, both on and off the field.

He made his first appearance for Borussia Dortmund's senior team at 17 years and 133 days old, becoming the eighth youngest player ever to appear in the Bundesliga. "It's a huge wave of emotions, nervousness, and excitement and everything flashes through you and you want to remember the moment," he said in a YouTube interview with VICE Sports about that game. That wave disappeared as soon he stepped onto the pitch. "Once you get on that field, it's gone, and you're just playing soccer like any other day."

Dortmund has arguably the best atmosphere in the Bundesliga. It's a wild riot of black and yellow flags and scarves and tens of thousands of fans jumping and singing in unison. When Pulisic scored his first goal for the team in April 2016, his dabbing goal celebration may have made him look like the kid he was, but he was also the new young favorite of the 80,000 fans in the stadium—an American teen crashing a German soccer party.

After his successful years at Dortmund, including winning the DFB-Pokal Cup in 2017, Pulisic signed to London's famed Premiership club, Chelsea, in January 2019 for a transfer equal to $73 million, a record amount for an American player. He was loaned back to Dortmund to finish the season but told talksport.com, "I'm excited to play alongside N'Golo Kanté. I think he's a fantastic player and I can't wait to meet him."

HOPE FOR U.S. SOCCER'S FUTURE

What makes Pulisic even more exciting is the potential he holds for the USMNT. He was named the 2017 USMNT player of the year, and had solid efforts in the United States's attempts to win the 2019 Gold Cup. He scored in the 6 to 0 trouncing of Trinidad and Tobago, captained the quarterfinal against Curaçao, and got a brace against Jamaica before the United States succumbed to its arch-rival, Mexico. He rounded out his summer break by starring in a commercial where he juggled his hometown's most famous product—a Hershey's Kiss—like a soccer ball.

Pulisic points to a hopeful future for the USMNT, as he and other players in his generation offer the possibility of a team of Americans that grew up immersed in American soccer. It's an exciting prospect.

FUN FACTS

⚽ Many American kids wear NBA jerseys, but how many American kids can claim NBA stars rep their jersey? A July 6, 2018, Instagram post by @bundesliga_en featured LeBron James sporting a Pulisic kit.

⚽ Pulisic broke Landon Donovan's youngest American Player of the Year record when he won the honor at age nineteen. He is also the youngest player to captain the USMNT side.

⚽ Born in Hershey, PA—"The Sweetest Place On Earth," and home to Hershey's Chocolate—Pulisic is a favorite of dad jokers everywhere any time he makes a "sweet" play.

It's All in the Family
THE HAZARD BROTHERS

Just before one of the 2018 World Cup qualifying games, Belgium football's official Twitter account posted, "#Hazard is the name, ⚽ is the game!" in honor of Belgian teammates and brothers, Thorgan and Eden Hazard. But the Hazard family has contributed more to soccer than just those two—there are *four* Hazard brothers, all playing soccer in what can only be called the family business.

The boys' father, Thierry, was an amateur player in the Belgian third division—but Eden says he takes after his mom, Carine. She played for Manage in the Belgian women's league. "I was in her stomach when she was playing . . . three months pregnant," jokes Eden, adding, "My dad played at the back, chilled out, calm on the ball. My mum was a striker."

Eden (following in his mother's footsteps as a forward) joined Real Madrid in June 2019, while Thorgan currently plays for Borussia Dortmund. The other two brothers are Kylian, who made his loan to Cercle Brugge permanent as of July 2019, and Ethan, who is a U17 player for Royal Stade Brainois. Eden, Thorgan, and Kylian played for Chelsea at one point, either as a senior team player or in the developmental program.

In a UEFA video portrait, Eden and Thorgan Hazard talked about the experience of playing together for Belgium's national team. "It's a pleasure," says Thorgan, "at first it feels a little weird being on the pitch together. But then you don't pay attention and you play as if it's just another player."

After a pause, he adds, "Okay, maybe sometimes you give him a few more passes," to which Eden protests, "You mustn't say that!" before they both smile and laugh.

Eden believes it's up to this incredible family to "continue working together to have fun . . . on a daily basis, in training, in games." The "creative spirit . . . forged in the garden between brothers" just might make a formidable Belgian team with as many as *four* Hazard brothers in the lineup. I can only imagine the fear that would strike the hearts of opponents.

However the Belgian team fares, one thing is certain: This is a family to watch.

★ LUKA MODRIĆ ★

Luka
MODRIĆ

10

POSITION: DEFENSIVE MIDFIELDER
CLUB TEAM: REAL MADRID C.F., LA LIGA
NATIONAL TEAM: CROATIA
HEIGHT: 5'8" – WEIGHT: 146 LBS
BORN: SEPTEMBER 9, 1985

- ✪ SPANISH CUP WINNER 13/14 REAL MADRID
- ✪ UEFA BEST PLAYER IN EUROPE 2018
- ✪ FIFA CLUB WORLD CUP WINNER 2014, 2016, 2017, 2018 REAL MADRID
- ✪ UEFA SUPERCUP WINNER 14/15, 16/17, 17/18

TRANSFERMARKT 2019 ESTIMATED VALUE:

$

22.3 MILLION

 @lukamodric10   @lukamodric10

How much would you have to love soccer to keep playing in a war zone as shells fell around you, forcing you to run for cover? That wasn't just a hypothetical question for Luka Modrić and was only part of his path to becoming a star for Real Madrid and the Croatian National Team.

Modrić was just a kid in a remote mountain region near Zaton Obrovacki when the Croatian War of Independence began. When his grandfather, also named Luka, was killed by the Serbian military and their family home was burned, the family fled to the city of Zadar and became refugees.

Modrić became known as the boy in the refugee hotel who was never without his soccer ball. He played with it in the hotel halls and took it to bed with him at night. When Josip Bajlo, the coach of the local club NK Zadar, saw Modrić play, he offered him a spot at the club's football school. Modrić was an instant hit with other kids in the program, who could immediately see how talented he was. Bajlo later said, "He was an idol to his generation . . . Already, children saw in him then what we are all seeing in him now."

Growing up surrounded by signs warning, "Mines – Keep Out!" and constant bombings gave Modrić a mental and physical toughness that has served him in his soccer career. A childhood friend (and fellow pro soccer player), Marijan Buljat,

remembers times when war threatened the young-
sters on their way to practices. "It happened a
million times that we were going to training as the
shells were falling and we were running to shelters,"
Buljat said, adding that he's certain it's "one of the
factors . . . that drove him [Modrić] to become one
of the best in the world."

The kids often had to abort training sessions at
Zadar to sprint for air-raid shelters to escape gre-
nades and mortars. Their coaches tried to keep things
fun by offering "hero of the day" awards to the fastest
kid to the shelter, but it must have been terrifying.

On the pitch itself, the young Modrić was not
the fastest player. Instead, what his coach Davorin
Matosevic noticed immediately was his ball con-
trol. "His touch was soft, velvety, and precise. For
a novice, it was amazing." There was, however, one
thing holding him back: his small size.

Zadar's youth coach, Miodrag Paunovic, recalls,
"At that time in the Balkans, the key idea was that
you had to be powerful to be a success in football.
For me, it was evident he [Modrić] was destined to
become great," although, "not many believed in
him because he was so thin and looked as delicate
as a leaf."

When he was twelve, Modrić was rejected by top
division club Hajduk Split, which told him to try
again in a year. He was devastated and considered

quitting, but another Zadar official—the head of the team's youth academy, Tomislav Bašić—saw his potential and mentored him. He helped Modrić find a trainer to bulk up his body and offered support and encouragement whenever it was needed. Modrić considered him a second father and dedicated his team's 2014 Champion's League win to the recently deceased Bašić, saying, "Without him, I wouldn't be where I am now."

Modrić was a "late bloomer." People were frustrated with his small size and lack of speed until, one day, he bloomed, and the world began to pay attention. He played in a tournament in Italy, where he attracted attention from Serie A clubs Parma, Inter Milan, and Juventus. Bašić, however, believed more time in Croatia would a better choice for Modrić.

He joined Dinamo Zagreb as a sixteen-year-old but struggled to find his place at the new club and in a city far away from his family. Zagreb loaned him to Zrinjski Mostar in the Bosnian Liga 12, known for its brute enforcers and tough guys. Surprisingly, Modrić continued to bloom both mentally and physically and was voted Player of the Year. Still unsure of where he fit with them, however, Zagreb then loaned Modrić to the Croatian team, Inter Zaprešić, where he again thrilled everyone around him, leading the squad to be the league's runner-up (for its first and only time) and getting called up to play on Croatia's U21 team.

Finally convinced of his value, Dinamo Zagreb signed a 10-year deal with Modrić, who used his earnings to buy his family an apartment in Zadar. After 13 years, the family finally had a home again and could turn in the keys to the refugee hotel.

Modrić didn't relax, though. He lit up Dinamo's attack, scoring 31 goals and racking up 29 assists on his way to three league wins, three domestic cup championships, and a Croatia National Team debut in 2006. One writer at the time called him "one of the best up-and-coming *trequartistas* in world football" (*trequartista* is an Italian word that means "three quarters," and it refers to a specialized player who shoots like a striker but is also a creative playmaker).

After Modrić spent some time with other European clubs, England's Tottenham Hotspur signed him to a six-year contract worth £16.5 million. He made 160 appearances for Tottenham, scoring 17 goals along the way, but he never won any hardware for the club. Just the same, most supporters enjoyed his visionary play and beautiful touch, and he helped them get their first Champions League appearance.

In August 2012, Modrić moved to Real Madrid for £30 million. In his seven years with the club, he has won 16 trophies, and, in 2018, he was named the

UEFA Best Player in Europe. When he arrived at the club, their powerful, established midfielders—Mesut Ozil, Xabi Alonso, and Sami Khedira—initially made it difficult for him to find his place, but as those three departed for other clubs, Modrić was able to create plays around his style and touch. As Sayan Chatterjee wrote for *El Arte Del Futbol,* "Modrić became the heartbeat of a Real Madrid side that made history."

A WORLD CUP TO END AN ERA

It was in the 2018 World Cup that Modrić truly altered history.

He led Croatia to the World Cup Final for the first time in their history. An article on FIFA.com declared, "Croatia owed their place in the Final in large part to their supremely gifted #10 [Modrić]. His two goals and one assist almost pale in comparison to his tireless work in the midfield, where he used his incisive vision to great effect in guiding his team, setting the tempo, and exploiting gaps in opposition defenses."

Although they ultimately lost to France, Modrić ended the decade-long stranglehold Cristiano Ronaldo and Lionel Messi had held on the Ballon d'Or.

Modrić was disappointed that his team didn't win the World Cup, but the Croatian press still loved him. In an article with a title that translates to, "Nothing is impossible for him, he surpassed even Suker!" Modrić is honored for winning Croatian Footballer of the Year a record-breaking seven times. Additionally, only Modrić and Ivica Olić have won both Footballer and Hope of the Year (Young Player).

FUN FACTS

- ⚽ Modrić is a dedicated family man. He married Vanja Bosnic in 2010 after they had dated for four years. They have two kids: Ivano and Ema. He's close with his childhood family, too, saying, "Not a day goes by when I don't speak to my parents and sisters back home."

- ⚽ The anti-discrimination Fare named him to their Refugee XI Team for 2016, 2017, 2018, and 2019. The list of refugee soccer players is generated annually in honor of World Refugee Day.

Honorable Mentions

MIDFIELDERS

KEVIN DE BRUYNE

When Kevin De Bruyne was eleven, he told his mom, "I want to study Latin for two years, then I'll go to Topsport School, and when I'm eighteen I will fully focus on my football." The young soccer-obsessed Belgian lived in soccer gear, slept in Liverpool bedding, and played the game as much as he was allowed. He and his buddies tore up the yard at a friend's house so much they were only allowed to use a plastic ball. The kids were able to bargain to play with a real ball once more if they only used their weaker foot. Today, the benefits of early training with his weaker side are easy to see.

After struggling early on with his reputation as a difficult character, De Bruyne has found his place at England's Premiership club Manchester City and on the Belgian national team. Man City's stress tests indicate that he is mostly "super chilled," with bottomed-out stress levels before matches. However, he can explode with a deeply stubborn passion for the game that occasionally requires his teammates to drag him away from on-field conflicts.

He is often featured on lists of the best players, including a 2017 ranking by the *Guardian* as fourth-best in the world, and he won Manchester City's own Player of the Year honor in both 2016 and 2018. He made the senior team in Belgium in 2010 and has since earned more than 70 caps and scored 16 goals for his country—including helping them reach the quarterfinals of the 2014 World Cup and winning the World Cup's third place match in 2018.

MESUT ÖZIL

Mesut Özil's club career at Schalke 04, Werder Bremen, Real Madrid, and Arsenal—while impressive—is less noteworthy than his accomplishments on the German national team. Sure, his transfer to Arsenal was the most expensive fee ever paid for a German player, but his status as the first German national team player from an immigrant background is helping cause a pivotal shift in German soccer culture.

In the United States, Özil would hardly be considered an immigrant as a third-generation, native-born German citizen. But in Germany, he's been so closely associated with his family's immigrant background that they often forget he was born in the country for which he plays. Sadly, according to *The*

Independent, he was too often "German when he won, an immigrant when he lost."

He was promoted to the German senior team in 2009 and was crucial in Germany's appearances in the 2010 World Cup, 2012 Euros, and 2016 Euros. He was the leading scorer in Germany's 2014 World Cup qualifying games and started all seven matches of the tournament on the team's path to being crowned champions. He scored the game-winning goal in the Round of 16 and played 120 minutes of the final.

You can imagine the shock, then, when Germany bombed out of the group stage of the Russia World Cup in 2018 with heartbreaking losses to Mexico and South Korea. Özil was targeted as a scapegoat for the team's failure because he had met with the Turkish President in London prior to the World Cup. The scrutiny became so intense that he announced his retirement, saying he would "no longer stand for being a scapegoat." It was a sad ending to a fantastic national team career.

As of this writing, Özil had missed Arsenal's opening match because of safety concerns after a recent attempted robbery at his home. Simultaneously, rumors swirl about a potential move for him to the United States and Major League Soccer. Wherever he ends up playing next, hopefully it's a place where the fans focus on his game and not on his family's background.

ARTURO VIDAL

Arturo Vidal plays as a midfielder for FC Barcelona and
the Chilean national team,
and his tattoos and
mohawk are a great
aesthetic for his
intensely aggressive
play. Game highlights
showcase deadly accuracy
when launching a pass
halfway up the field—not to mention his sneaky
back heel. His goals that aren't headers are usually
either a casual classic tap-in with his instep or a
strange flying kick that looks more like an awkward
attempt at a can-can dance than a soccer kick, but it
works with surprising consistency and makes him
an exciting player to watch.

He started with Chilean Pimera League side
Colo-Colo, where he won three league titles.
Germany's Bayer Leverkusen brought him
to Europe in 2007, where he was a standout
midfielder. He moved to Italian side Juventus in
2011, and won the "Scudetto" (the Serie A league
championship) in each of his four seasons there.
He then headed back to Germany with Bayern
Munich and added three Bundesliga titles to

his list of trophies. In 2018, he joined Barcelona, where he made his debut game as a substitute in his team's 2018 Spanish Super Cup win. Four countries, four championships—it's a pretty impressive record.

He has 113 caps and 27 goals for Chile to date, including appearances in the 2011, 2015, and 2019 Copa America tournament, and in the Copa America Centenario in 2016. He was a part of Chile's 2010 World Cup team that advanced out of their group only to face Brazil (and lose) in the Round of 16; he was also an often-starting member of their 2014 World Cup team that again advanced to face Brazil in the Round of 16, only to lose to them again, this time in penalties.

DIEGO VALERI

I must give a shout-out to my favorite member of the Portland Timbers, Argentine national Diego Valeri. Personally, I think the Timbers were and are the greatest team in Major League Soccer before, during, and after their 2015 Championship season. If watching the smooth, creative playmaking of Valeri doesn't make you happy, watching his daughter's irresistible postgame on-camera interviews surely will. Plus, he scored the fastest goal in MLS Cup history just 27 seconds after kick-off.

Gamechanger

DAVID BECKHAM

David Beckham had a fantastic career for England and his club teams before ever joining Major League Soccer:

- ⚽ He's the first English player to win the league in four countries: at home in England with Manchester United, in Spain for Real Madrid, in the United States with LA Galaxy, and finally with Paris Saint-Germain in France.

- ⚽ He represented England for 13 years through highs and lows, retiring as the second most capped player in England's history (although he's subsequently been demoted to third by Wayne Rooney).

- ⚽ He was the first English player to score in three separate World Cups and was runner up for FIFA World Player of the Year twice (1999, 2001).

David Beckham's career was epic on many levels, but I chose him because of the impact he had on Major League Soccer in the United States.

When he joined the league in 2007, MLS added the Designated Player Rule (nicknamed the Beckham Rule) so MLS clubs could afford the likes of his higher-valued contract. This rule allows MLS clubs to sign up to three players whose contracts are above the league's salary cap, either with a higher salary or transfer fee.

Adding Beckham to the league gave it a new credibility, increasing attendance, raising television value, and adding legitimacy to a league that had previously been known as something of a "retirement league" for international superstars. During Beckham's five-year tenure, the league expanded from 12 to 22 teams, and attendance more than doubled overall. Some of that growth certainly would have happened *without* Beckham, but he forced changes in the league that were required to take it to the next level.

And if it wasn't enough that Beckham was a great athlete, he is married to a Spice Girl, is an occasional model for high-end fashion designers, and is friendly with plenty of Hollywood movie stars. That, too, has helped infuse soccer into American culture. *Sports Illustrated* soccer writer, Grant Wahl, sums it up well, saying, "He was still a bit more successful as a celebrity than as a soccer player, which makes sense, because we're more of a celebrity culture than a soccer culture."

PARIS SAINT GERMAIN FC (PSG)

★ KYLIAN MBAPPÉ ★

Kylian MBAPPÉ

7

POSITION: FORWARD
CLUB TEAM: PARIS SAINT-GERMAIN FC (PSG)
NATIONAL TEAM: FRANCE
HEIGHT: 5'10" – WEIGHT: 172 LBS
BORN: DECEMBER 20, 1998

- ⚽ FRENCH CHAMPION: 17/18, 18/19 PSG, 16/17 AS MONACO
- ⚽ FRENCH CUP WINNER: 17/18
- ⚽ FRENCH LEAGUE CUP WINNER: 17/18
- ⚽ EUROPEAN U19 CHAMPION: 2016

TRANSFERMARKT 2019 ESTIMATED VALUE:

$

270 MILLION

 @KMbappe   @k.mbappe

When people think of the GOAT (greatest of all time) soccer players, Pelé, the famous Brazilian player of the 1960s and 1970s, always comes to mind. So, when there's a modern player setting Pelé-esque records, he absolutely warrants a spot on this fantasy team.

It was at the 2018 World Cup when the young Frenchman Kylian Mbappé became the second teenager (after Pelé) to score in a World Cup Final. He helped his team win the World Cup Tournament as the co-second highest goal scorer and won Best Young Player at the tournament.

But let's not get too far ahead of ourselves.

Mbappé was born in Paris, France, into a sports-loving family. His mom, Fayza Lamari, is a former Division 1 handball player, and his dad, Wilfried Mbappé, is a soccer coach and serves as Kylian's agent. His brother Ethan plays for Paris Saint-Germain FC's U12 team, and his other brother Jirès is a professional footballer with Buraspur in Turkey.

His early coaches could see there was something special about Mbappé right from the start. Even when he was a six-year-old playing for his dad, who coached the local club for the Parisian suburb where he lived (AS Bondy) the other coaches were impressed. Then president of AS Bondy, Atmane

Airouche, said, "He's got eyes in the back of his head. He knows how to anticipate where the ball will go."

Mbappé says, "A place like Bondy simply has values you keep wherever you go." Respect others, remain humble, love football. Today, there is a five-story mural in his old suburban neighborhood, visible from the main road; it's a portrait of Mbappé signing, "I love you," and it reads, in French, "Bondy, the City of Possibilities."

As he continued to develop as a player, Mbappé landed at the Clairefontaine Academy and began to attract the attention of top clubs like Real Madrid, Chelsea, Liverpool, Manchester City, and Bayern Munich. When he was eleven years old, he went for a trial with Chelsea. He eventually joined Monaco instead, making his first Ligue 1 appearance just 18 days shy of his seventeenth birthday. Coming in as a substitute in that match broke the record that French legend, Thierry Henry, set 21 years earlier as the youngest first-team player. Mbappé also broke Henry's record as Monaco's youngest goal scorer when he scored his first goal for the club the following February at age seventeen (and 62 days). In March, the club signed him to a 3-year contract, and he still hadn't turned eighteen yet.

CRITICAL HITS

⚽ Dec 14, 2016: First hat trick in Coupe de la League (first for the club in that competition since 1997).

⚽ Feb 11, 2017: First hat trick in Ligue 1 making him the youngest hat trick scorer in Ligue 1.

⚽ Feb 21, 2017: First goal in UEFA Champions League.

⚽ 2016–17 season: Mbappé continued to be a phenomenon for Monaco, advancing his team to the UEFA Champions League semi-finals, and helping Monaco win the Ligue 1 title, scoring 26 goals in his 44 appearances.

Mbappé's stellar performance in the 2016–17 season in Monaco did not go unnoticed. By the end of August 2017, Paris Saint-Germain (PSG) had signed Mbappé on loan in a deal reported at €180 million. It was the highest amount ever paid for a teenager and second only to what PSG spent on Brazilian phenomenon, Neymar, who was purchased earlier that same summer for €220 million.

In May 2018, Mbappé had been so successful at PSG that the club's President, Nasser Al-Khelaifi, quipped, "If you gave me a billion euros, I wouldn't sell him." Mbappé scored in his first game with PSG, then scored again four days later in an away UEFA Champions League match at Scotland's Celtic. By December 6 of that year, he had scored 10 Champions League goals, becoming the youngest player to do so. PSG won the French league title and the Coupe de France (French Cup) in Mbappé's first season with the club.

The 2018–19 season brought even more records. Mbappé became the youngest player (19.75 years) to score four goals in a Ligue 1 match, and it only took him 13 minutes to do it. The fifth goal PSG scored in that game was connected to Mbappé, too, since it was a penalty kick Neymar scored after Mbappé had been fouled in the box. He was awarded the FIFA 2018 Young Player of the Year and the inaugural Kopa Trophy, given to the best male player under the age of 21.

A PELÉ SHOUT-OUT

Playing for France on the U19 squad, Mbappé scored five of the team's goals during the 2016 UEFA European U19 Championship tournament. He scored a brace in the semifinal 3 to 1 win over Portugal.

He was only eighteen years, three months, and five days old when he debuted for the senior France team on March 25, 2017, making him the second-youngest French player ever. He scored his first senior team goal against the Netherlands on August 31, 2017, in a World Cup qualifier and earned himself a spot on the French World Cup roster.

The 2018 World Cup was near perfection for France, and Mbappé was a huge part of that. He became the youngest French goal scorer when he scored against Peru in the group stage. He earned Man of the Match honors with his two goals (and he drew a penalty for a third) against Argentina. To top it all off, at the conclusion of the tournament, in addition to helping lift the trophy for France, he was crowned FIFA World Cup Best Young Player.

And throughout it all, he remained grounded. When asked about making history as the second teen to score in a World Cup after Pelé, Mbappé responded, "It's flattering to be the second one after Pelé but let's put things into context—Pelé is in another category." Pelé responded via a tweet: "Only the second teenager to have scored a goal in a #WorldCupFinal! Welcome to the club, @KMbappe—it's great to have some company!"

Mbappé's fame has meant so much to the kids in the immigrant neighborhood where he grew up. One of the moms at AS Bondy, Fatounaia Dabo, said, "Our children suffer because we have no hope. When they come home, they asked us, 'Even if we work, mommy, it's not possible for us to be lawyers and doctors. We are really French. Why is it like this?' Now, Kylian has changed the way they see things."

FUN FACTS

⚽ Mbappé could have played for three different national teams. His mother is of Algerian descent, and his father is from Cameroon. But Kylian always wanted to play for the nation of his own birth, France.

⚽ He donated all of his World Cup pay to charity. He thought the honor of playing for his country was enough of a reward and donated his estimated €400,000 (almost half a million US dollars) to the children's charity Premiers de Cordée.

⚽ His trademark arms-crossed goal celebration is an imitation of his brother's taunts when he wins on the FIFA video game.

⚽ As a kid, his nickname was Beep-Beep, after the Road Runner from *Looney Tunes*.

⚽ He has more Instagram followers than the French president (34.8 million as of this writing).

Spotlight
SOCCER SUPPORTERS

There are several different names for people who enjoy watching soccer. People who are casual soccer enthusiasts might be called fans, but as you become more interested in soccer, you may hear terms like "supporter," "ultra," or even "hooligan."

Supporters are usually fans who do extra things to show their love for their club. Ultra is another word for supporter, but implies the most passionate, devoted fan of the team. Hooligan can sometimes be used as a derogatory term for supporters, since it implies the impish and sometimes violent trouble-making behavior that soccer fans (particularly in Europe) were once known for.

In the United States, terms like "ultra" and "hooligan" have been imported from foreign soccer cultures—though most of the nastiness associated with them has not. In fact, when my family and I started traveling to follow the US national team, people would ask us if we were worried about the hooligans. I would jokingly answer, "No, *we* are the hooligans!"

Supporters form groups to support their teams. This can be an especially interesting part of soccer culture, and I try to learn about a team's supporters groups when I travel to watch games.

For my local club, the Des Moines Menace, I am part of what's called the "Red Army"—the oldest supporters club in the USL 2 league. For my MLS club, the Portland Timbers, there is one main supporters group called the "Timbers Army," but that group is further broken down into stadium sections, each with their own unique style. When I visit Portland, I sit in Timbers Army section 104 with what's known as "Charlie Company." Not only that, as a member of the Timbers Army living in Iowa, I am also part of the "Timbers Army, Heartland Regiment."

We all enjoy spending time with people who share our interests, and these supporters groups allow soccer fans to do that in different ways.

SUPPORTERS GLOSSARY

SG/SC: Short for Supporters Group or Supporters Club.

Capo: Some clubs have "capos," or song leaders, who will stand at the front of a fan section and lead supporters in coordinated cheers, songs, and clapping rhythms. Capos must be aware of what's happening in the game while also paying attention to the crowd to make sure everyone is appropriately excited and loud at the right times—all this when they often have their backs to the field! It may take a certain amount of bravery to lead a stadium section's chants and songs, but it's an honor in most groups to be a capo, and many hold their positions for years.

Tifo: Short for "tifosi," tifo is the term used in the United States for the large painted or printed banners that are displayed usually just before the start of a game. Tifos show support for the home team or mock the opponent—or both. Many tifos are inspired by pop culture or include clever references to the teams or game. An away game tifo might be as small as 8-by-12 feet, but a home game tifo can be huge and cover multiple stadium sections.

Banner: Many supporters groups, especially regional national team groups, will have a banner with their name to hang along the bottom of their section in the stadium. Sometimes clubs have banners for subgroups, special events, or individual players.

Two-Stick: A two-stick is a smaller version of a tifo, similar in size to a banner, but created to be supported by two poles (usually PVC pipe), hence the name. It is held up before and sometimes during the game to show support for the team, a particular player, or an event.

Flags: Supporters sometimes wave flags of either their country, their city, or their team's colors. They can make a supporters section look like an ocean of waves when enough of them are waving at the same time.

WHAT SUPPORTERS DO

Different clubs have different cultures and traditions, with the most visible being how they support the team during a game. Generally, clubs will sing, cheer, clap, and make noise for their team throughout the game. Most supporters groups stand for the entire match. They will make visual displays of support using tifos, banners, flags, and other creative displays.

Groups often have a name for the section of the stadium in which they sit. The supporters for Kansas City's Sporting KC call their section "The Cauldron," a reference to when the team was called the KC Wizards. New England Revolution's Midnight Riders sit in "The Fort." And the Chicago Fire has "Section 8," named for the original section where supporters groups would sit in the stadium.

In addition to their presence at games, some supporters clubs have social or charitable events throughout the year. For instance, New England's Midnight Riders have had a golf outing that supports their charities, and the Timbers Army has several different charitable projects their members can participate in (earning limited-run patches for their volunteer work).

US SOCCER GROUPS

Having a supporters group for a national team can be a bit trickier than a club team because the fans for a national team are spread across the entire country, which is even more challenging when you're talking about a big country like the United States.

Organized support for US soccer began in 1995 with Sam's Army, a group that was born during the 1994 World Cup (hosted by the United States). By 2010, Sam's Army claimed 14,000 members but struggled to organize in cities without MLS teams.

In 2007, a new group calling themselves the "American Outlaws" formed in Lincoln, Nebraska, under the motto "Unite and Strengthen." This group had a structure that made it much easier to organize in smaller markets. While they remain the largest US national team supporters group today with more than 30,000 members, they've suffered some growing pains. This led to the launch of Sammers SC, a group that is more focused on the in-stadium experience of soccer, with the motto "We Sing for 90."

There isn't necessarily a rivalry between these supporters groups, however. In fact, there are many who can claim membership in *all three* of these supporters groups—including this author.

★ RAHEEM STERLING ★

Raheem
STERLING

7

POSITION: MIDFIELDER
CLUB TEAM: MANCHESTER CITY, PREMIER
NATIONAL TEAM: ENGLAND
HEIGHT: 5'7" – WEIGHT: 152 LBS
BORN: DECEMBER 8, 1994

⚽ **ENGLISH CHAMPION 2018, 2019 MANCHESTER CITY**

⚽ **ENGLISH FA CUP WINNER 2019 MANCHESTER CITY**

⚽ **ENGLISH LEAGUE CUP WINNER 2016, 2018, 2019 MANCHESTER CITY**

TRANSFERMARKT 2019 ESTIMATED VALUE:

$

159.6 MILLION

 @sterling7   **@sterling7**

In a video interview with *The Players' Tribune*, Raheem Sterling talks about growing up in the shadow of the legendary Wembley Stadium. As a kid playing soccer in the neighborhood, he said, "I'd turn and the arches [of the stadium] would be literally over my head." Games at the stadium made an even bigger impression on the young Sterling. "When they were playing you could *hear* the goals," he said. "You could watch the game [on TV] and just turn the volume off." He told his friends, "One day I'm going to be king of that stadium."

But Sterling didn't get his start in England. He was born in Kingston, Jamaica, where his father was murdered when Raheem was just two years old. "That shaped my entire life," Sterling said. His mother then traveled alone to England to get her degree and improve things for the family while Raheem and his sister stayed behind in Jamaica with their grandmother.

"Thank God I had football," Sterling writes of that period in *The Players' Tribune*. "I remember when it used to rain, all the kids would run outside and play football in the puddles. That's the image that flashes in my mind when I think about the atmosphere of Jamaica. When it rains, nobody hides inside. You just go out and enjoy it."

When Sterling was five, he and his sister moved to England, where they were finally reunited with their mother. He remembers going with his mother to the hotel where she worked as a cleaner to pay her college tuition—getting up at 5:00 a.m. and fighting his sister to help make hotel beds or scrub toilets.

He was a bit of a troublemaker in school until he met a neighborhood mentor, Clive Ellington, who asked, "Raheem, what do you *love* to do?" The answer, "I love playing football," came easily to Sterling.

Ellington had a Sunday League team and offered the boy a spot. "That moment changed my life," says Sterling. "From that day, it was football, football, football." Big clubs took an interest, even when he was just ten or eleven, but his mom cautioned, "If you go [to a big club like Arsenal] there's going to be 50 players who are just as good as you. You'll just be a number. You need to go somewhere you can work your way up."

So, with the help of his family, he joined London's Queens Park Rangers. "My mum would never let me go to training alone . . . so my sister would have to take me. [It took us] three buses [to get there.] We'd leave at 3:15 and get home at 11. Every. Single. Day." That's pretty impressive sibling support from his seventeen-year-old sister.

At fourteen, Sterling was messing around at school and his teacher scolded him, telling him that millions of kids want to be professional footballers—a hint that simply wanting it wasn't a guarantee that it would happen. As he remembers it, "Two months later, I got called up to the England U16s, and I set up two goals against Northern Ireland. It was all on television and everything." When he returned to school, that teacher had suddenly become his best friend.

Liverpool FC came calling when Sterling was fifteen. He moved in with a couple in their 70s who hosted him on behalf the club and he—as he put it—"went ghost," leaving his friends and family behind to focus on becoming a famous football star in order to make it big and eventually help his family financially. He followed through with that goal, too; his mom had to move many times by the time he got his Liverpool contract, so he bought a house for her.

Sterling stayed at Liverpool until 2015 and on October 20, 2012, became the second youngest player to score for them in a competitive match. He was shortlisted for PFA Young Player of the Year in 2014 and took home both Liverpool's Young Player of the Year and the 2014 Golden Boy Award.

In 2015, Sterling and Liverpool got into a nasty contract dispute. The club said they had offered him "an incredible deal," and he rejected it. "It's never been about money," said Sterling of the disagreement in an interview with the BBC. "I talk about winning trophies throughout my career. That's all I talk about." The club was furious and forced Manchester

City, the club that was interested in Sterling, into a bidding war before finally approving the transfer for a "most expensive English player of all time" record £44 million with £5 million of possible add-ons.

He's gotten past all of that and found success at Man City, making 132 appearances and scoring 51 goals to date. After less than three weeks with the team, he had already scored his first hat trick, and, on his birthday that year, he scored a brace in the final 10 minutes of Man City's last group stage match of the UEFA Champions League tournament.

FROM NEIGHBORHOOD KID TO WEMBLEY STAR

Sterling got the call up to the senior England side when he was just seventeen, and his first international game was a World Cup Qualifier against Ukraine at Wembley—the stadium that loomed, literally, over his childhood. He says it was surreal to drive through his old neighborhood on the team bus. He looked out the window, thinking, "That's the house where my friend used to live. That's the parking lot where we used to roller skate. That's the green where I used to dream that all of this was going to happen."

For Sterling, England was "still a place where a naughty boy who comes from nothing can live his dream."

FIGHTING RACISM

In December 2018, Sterling became an outspoken advocate against racism following incidents directed at him during a match at Chelsea and another at a Spurs vs. Arsenal match. Sterling took to Instagram to respond to both and used the platform to show how black and white players were portrayed differently by the English media.

The Instagram post shows two stories in the *Daily Mail* about young players—Sterling and a white player named Phil Foden—buying houses for their mothers. The headline about Sterling's purchase never even mentioned his mother and shamed him for spending so much on a house "despite never having started a Premier League match." The headline about Foden's purchase, however, put the youngster on a pedestal: "Manchester City starlet Phil Foden buys new £2m home for his mum."

"I think this [is] unacceptable," wrote Sterling in the caption accompanying the images. "[I] have not done a thing wrong but just by the way it has been worded. This young black kid is looked at in a bad light. Which helps fuel racism an aggressive behaviour, so for all the newspapers that don't understand why people are racist in this day and age all I have to say is have a second thought about fair publicity an give all players an equal chance."

Sterling later corresponded with a young fan, Ethan Ross, who wrote to him about facing racism at school. He sent the boy a letter of support that was turned into an inspirational mural at Ethan's school. Ethan also got to spend time with Sterling and tour Manchester City grounds. Sterling was awarded the Integrity and Impact award in April 2019 for his efforts to fight racism.

FUN FACTS

- ⚽ Sterling has a unique running style, which he described in a 2014 *COPA90* interview: "I know I've got the T-Rex arms—I get [teased] for it all of the time but it's not a problem for me as long as I'm either scoring or doing something right!"

- ⚽ His birthday is the same as Nicki Minaj, Mary Queen of Scots, and the author of this book—we were all born on December 8.

- ⚽ His daughter, Melody Rose, born in 2012, occasionally makes appearances on his Instagram.

LIVERPOOL

★ SADIO MANÉ ★

Sadio
MANÉ

10

POSITION: FORWARD
CLUB TEAM: LIVERPOOL
NATIONAL TEAM: SENEGAL
HEIGHT: 5'9" – WEIGHT: 152 LBS
BORN: APRIL 10, 1992

- ⚽ UEFA SUPERCUP 19/20 LIVERPOOL FC
- ⚽ TOP SCORER 18/19 LIVERPOOL FC
- ⚽ PREMIER LEAGUE TOP SCORER 18/19
- ⚽ CHAMPIONS LEAGUE WINNER
  18/19 LIVERPOOL FC
- ⚽ AUSTRIAN CHAMPION 13/14,
  14/15 RED BULL SALZBURG

$ TRANSFERMARKT 2019 ESTIMATED VALUE:

136.8 MILLION

 @10SadioMane   **@sadiomaneofficiel**

Liverpool produces fun get-to-know-the-players videos on their YouTube channel, including a few about forward, Sadio Mané. There's a fun one called, "Bezzies with Salah and Mané," in which he and teammate, Mo Salah, answer silly questions about each other.

When asked about each other's best mate on the team, Salah said he really likes Mané and that "Sadio is more quiet, he talks when he wants." Salah is then asked who Mané's best mate is, to which he laughs and replies, "No one—Sadio's living alone in Europe."

Mané laughs, too, and confirms, "I'm not someone who loves talking too much." He does, however, go on to talk about how he likes to help new players learn their way around and get settled. He comes across as a quiet, shy person who is funny and supportive when needed. In another interview with *Bleacher Report*, Mané said that while much of the focus is on the team's superstars (himself and Salah), "The strength of Liverpool is the collective. You can't forget that there's a guy up front called Firmino who works like an animal for us. The guys behind us do some extraordinary work. We try to benefit from that and help the team forward."

Mané was born in Senegal and was ten years old when his country made a surprising run to the 2002 World Cup quarter finals. Two stars on that

2002 team, Salif Diao and El-Hadji Diouf, both played from Liverpool. "They really inspired me," Mané later said. "Those two players were examples for me as a footballer. They were skillful players and good dribblers who beat their opponents easily."

Mané played wherever and whenever he could as a child. "I started playing in the streets and on a pitch in my home village," he says. "It wasn't the best pitch, but we tried to make do because that's the kind of pitch you find where I'm from." Today, Mané works to make sure opportunities are available for kids coming up behind him. He donated £200,000 to build a school in his home village, saying he has "lots of projects under way." As those projects become reality, he hopes they will allow for "other Sadio Manés" in the future.

Having grown up playing on the streets and in the sand, fifteen-year-old Mané made the transition to the next level in soccer by leaving his family—without telling anyone—and setting off on a 500-mile journey to Dakar for soccer tryouts. Unsurprisingly, his mother was not happy about him running away and sent his brother to retrieve him so he could finish school.

Once he had completed his studies, however, his family realized they weren't going to talk him out of his dream of becoming a footballer, so they let him go to tryouts. The club organizer thought he was in the wrong place because he didn't have proper soccer shorts and his shoes were very old and torn. Mané told the coach that it was the best equipment he owned and he just wanted a chance to play.

Once Mané took to the field, the coach couldn't hide his surprise. "I'm picking you straight away," he announced. "You'll play in my team." After that (and some work convincing his family), Mané had a place in the academy at Generation Foot, a Sengalese program for developing soccer players. He was signed to Metz in France at age nineteen.

HAT TRICK MAESTRO

After about eight months and 22 appearances in Metz, Mané was transferred to the Austrian Bundesliga club Red Bull Salzburg in August 2012. He signed with Southampton in the English Premiership in 2014, and then moved to Liverpool FC in 2016. His overall record is impressive, but one statistic stands out—his hat tricks.

Scoring three goals in one game is no easy feat, but Mané has done it numerous times. In 87 appearances with Salzburg, he scored 45 goals—including three hat tricks. With Southampton, he set a new league record for the fastest hat trick when he scored three goals in the space of less than three minutes. During his second season at Southampton, he had one hat trick among his 15 goals.

In June 2016, Mané's £34 million transfer to Liverpool made him the most expensive African player. Coach Jürgen Klopp first showed interest while he was coaching at Dortmund and Mané was playing in Salzburg, but Mané said, "Things didn't work out back then and it was frustrating, but that's life—nothing just comes easily. I told myself to just carry on working hard, push myself and something big would come. I did that. I went to Southampton, I played well and then, Klopp wanted me again. Now I'm lucky enough to be working with one of the best managers in football. It was meant to happen, and I am very happy to be learning all the time from him."

Mané really values what he learns from those around him. "When you're a little boy, sometimes you think you know everything about football," he says. "You want to do it your way. But I have learnt so many different styles, different tactical things, and how to be a more complete player from my days at the academy until now, with the help of great coaches and teammates."

Mané was part of the 2012 Olympic team for Senegal that advanced out of their group only to fall in extra time in the quarterfinals to the eventual champion, Mexico. Following that tournament as a U23 player, he joined the senior Senegal side and currently stands at 62 caps and 18 goals with his national team. He played in the 2015 and 2017 editions of the Africa Cup of Nations and scored the opening goal against Japan in Senegal's 2018 World Cup effort.

FUN FACTS

- ⚽ Sadio Mané is a practicing Muslim.

- ⚽ His parents didn't know much about soccer, but his uncle and the people in his village saw his talent and helped raise money for him to play soccer.

- ⚽ Mané has many siblings, and there wasn't money for him to go to school. Instead, he played soccer all the time.

Honorable Mentions
FORWARDS

EDIN DŽEKO

Džeko plays in the Italian Serie A for AS Roma and is the captain of the national team of Bosnia and Herzegovina. He earned the nickname "Bosnian Diamond" for his brilliant play, and he's the first player to get 100 caps for Bosnia. He's also a top goal scorer for Roma.

While playing at Manchester City earlier in his career, Džeko became the first member of that team to score four goals in a Premier League match, and that included what's called a "perfect hat trick" (scoring one goal each with the left foot, right foot, and head). When he became the top goal scorer for Bosnia, he did it with style—a hat trick brought his total to 24, two more than the previous Bosnian record.

Džeko is a well-rounded guy, too. He is fluent in several languages: Czech, German, English, Italian, and his native Bosnian. My favorite quote of his is, "I always try my best. Sometimes that's enough to get a good result, sometimes not, but I never give up and never will." That's something we can all take to heart.

MOHAMED "MO" SALAH

Mo Salah is basically wonderful, and it was a toss-up between him and Mané for which epic Liverpool forward would be featured. Salah blew up social media during the summer of 2019 with stories of going back to check on—and pose for photos with—one of his young Liverpool fans who had broken his nose in a fall while chasing after Mo's car.

Salah also plays on the Egyptian national team. He won BBC African Footballer of the Year in both 2017 and 2018, and Liverpool supporters have a great song they sing for him called, "Mo Salah, The Egyptian King." Raheem Sterling even talks about his own little girl running around their house and singing about Salah.

I loved the interview on YouTube called "When Mo Salah met Gary Lineker" and recommend you check it out. He talks about his four-hour commute to soccer practice and the challenges of playing in a foreign country. It's inspiring.

JADON SANCHO

Jadon Sancho is a winger for Germany's Borussia
Dortmund and the English national team. He was
born in England to parents from Trinidad and
Tobago. He loved playing soccer in the streets of
his native London but ended up joining a club in
Watford when he was seven years old. "What might
have happened if I hadn't [focused on soccer] is
with me all the time," he said of the somewhat
sketchy neighborhood in which he grew up.

At the tender age of nineteen, he has already
made 47 appearances for Borussia Dortmund and
six for the senior England squad after winning the
FIFA U17 World Cup in 2017. One can only assume
big things are ahead for this young player.

The Rivalry That Changed the Game

MESSI VS. RONALDO

In other sections of this book, I've chosen one legendary player to represent different positions on the field. But there is simply no way to have only one legendary player in the position of forward. Why? Because the soccer world is currently living in the era of two icons playing the game at the same time—two names that will be remembered decades from now.

It's like candy for fans.

Lionel Messi and Cristiano Ronaldo have been battling for the (informal) title of greatest soccer forward since 2007 in both international (Argentina and Portugal, respectively) and club games (currently Barcelona and Juventus, respectively, although up until 2018, these two heightened the rivalry that is Barcelona versus Real Madrid when Ronaldo played for the latter).

They are tied at five Ballon d'Ors each. There is an entire website devoted solely to their running stats (messivsronaldo.net). The F2Freestylers—Ultimate Soccer Skills Channel on YouTube has done two videos comparing competitive stats between the two players set to skill demos that will blow your mind (and they've garnered a combined 77 million views). There is even more in-depth statistical analysis to be found on michelacosta .com/en/messi-vs-ronaldo/, where you can compare these two players in every imaginable way.

CREATE YOUR OWN FANTASY TEAM

You can use this diagram to create your own fantasy team. Or, better yet, make some copies of this page and have your friends create their own teams, too, then compare to see who everyone picked.

References

"Afcon 2015: Yaya Toure Hails 'Unbelievable' Ivory Coast Win." *BBC*. February 9, 2015. https://www.bbc.com/sport /football/31271441.

Ames, Nick. "Christian Pulisic: The Making of a Young Man Ready to Step Up." *The Guardian*. May 31, 2016. https://www.theguardian .com/football/blog/2016/may/31/christian-pulisic-usa-soccer -copa-america-2016.

"Arturo Vidal." *Wikipedia*. Accessed August 11, 2019. https:// en.wikipedia.org/wiki/Arturo_Vidal.

Balagué, Guillem. "Exclusive Interview: Guillem Balagué Speaks with Spurs' Hugo Lloris." *Diario AS*. October 31, 2017. https://en.as .com/en/2017/10/31/football/1509440208_778065.html.

Barve, Abhijeet. "Sergio Ramos: A Remarkable Story of Light and Dark." *Football Paradise*. May 31, 2017. https://www.football paradise.com/sergio-ramos/.

Belgian Red Devils. "Brothers in Arms @UEFAcom Made a Portrait about @HazardEden10 & @HazardThorgan8." *Twitter*. August 19, 2019. https://twitter.com/BelRedDevils /status/1163387477232705536.

Bidwell, Nick. "Europe's Best Midfielder: Luka Modric Biography." *World Soccer*. September 18, 2018. https://www.worldsoccer.com /features/luka-modric-396393.

Bienkowski, Stefan. "German When He Won, an Immigrant When He Lost - Why Mesut Ozil Turned His Back on Germany." *The Independent*. July 23, 2018. https://www.independent.co.uk /sport/football/international/mesut-ozil-erdogan-retires-news -reinhard-grindel-racism-arsenal-a8459651.html.

Bilger, Phillipe. "Hugo Lloris: Un Dernier Rempart." *Justice au Singulier*. April 2, 2010. https://www.philippebilger.com /blog/2010/04/hugo-lloris-un-dernier-rempart.html.

BloodsugarNatz. "The Player Behind the Name: Sadio Mané, Part One." *The Liverpool Offside*. February 18, 2018. https://

liverpooloffside.sbnation.com/2018/2/18/17024898/the-player
-behind-the-name-sadio-mane-part-one-liverpool-champions
-league-premier-league.

"Boulogne vs. Monaco 1 - 2." *Soccerway*. 2012. https://int.soccerway
.com/matches/2012/05/18/france/ligue-2/union-sportive-de
-boulogne-cote-dopale/association-sportive-monaco-fc/1115476/.

Bourne, Diane. "Paddy McGuinness, Yaya Toure and Michael
Owen Join Soccer Aid Line-Up." *Manchester Evening News*. April 9,
2018. https://www.manchestereveningnews.co.uk/whats-on/family
-kids-news/paddy-mcguinness-toure-soccer-aid-14508633.

Brown, Nick. "10 Things You Need to Know About Edin Dzeko."
Official AS Roma Website. August 12, 2015. https://www.asroma
.com/en/news/2015/08/10-things-you-need-to-know-about
-edin-dzeko.

Bruce, Skye Eddy. "Kelley Pulisic – On the Importance of Free
Play." *Soccer Parenting Association*. March 15, 2017. https://www
.soccerparenting.com/kelley-pulisic-importance-free-play/.

Cassin, Elizabeth. "Faster than Usain Bolt?" *BBC*. November 21,
2015. https://www.bbc.com/news/magazine-34884849.

Chatterjee, Sayan. "Luka Modric: Dancing With The Devils From
Zadar to Madrid." *El Arte Del Futbol*. September 4, 2018. https://
www.elartedf.com/modric-story-zadar-madrid/.

"Christian Pulisic - Titles & Victories." *Transfermarkt*. 2019.
https://www.transfermarkt.com/christian-pulisic/erfolge
/spieler/315779.

"Christian Pulisic." *Wikipedia*. Accessed August 3, 2019. https://
en.wikipedia.org/wiki/Christian_Pulisic.

**"Christian Pulisic: 10 Things You Might Not Know about
Borussia Dortmund's USA Star."** *Bundesliga*. Accessed
August 27, 2018. https://www.bundesliga.com/en/news
/Bundesliga/christian-pulisic-10-things-on-borussia-dortmund
-s-nascent-usa-star-459300.jsp.

Connolly, Kate. "Immigration: The Rare Success Story of Mesut
Ozil." *The Guardian*. November 15, 2010. https://www.theguardian
.com/world/2010/nov/15/mesut-ozil-turkish-german-football.

Corrigan, Dermont. "Sergio Ramos Reaches 150 Caps for Spain: Six of His Best Appearances." *ESPN*. March 24, 2018. https://www.espn.co.uk/football/club/spain/164/blog/post/3430108/sergio-ramos-150-spain-caps-highlights-of-remarkable-international-career.

Corrigan, Dermot. "Sergio Ramos Red Card Record at Real Madrid: All 25 Sendings Off." *ESPN*. February 17, 2019. https://www.espn.com/soccer/spanish-primera-division/15/blog/post/3297210/sergio-ramos-red-card-record-at-real-madrid-all-25-sendings-off.

Culliford, Graeme. "Bitter Split: Ex-Celtic Ace Virgil van Dijk Dropped Dad's Name from Shirt Over Family Feud." *The Scottish Sun*. January 13, 2018. https://www.thescottishsun.co.uk/news/2089460/virgil-van-dijk-celtic-liverpool-football-family-feud-dad/.

Dasović, Tomislav. "Za Njega Ništa Nije Nemoguće, Nadmašio Je Čak i Šukera!" *Večernji list*. December 24, 2018. https://www.vecernji.hr/sport/za-njega-nista-nije-nemoguce-nadmasio-je-cak-i-sukera-1290705.

Dean, Sam. "Hugo Lloris: 'After France's World Cup Win I Felt so Empty.'" *The Telegraph*. February 9, 2019. https://www.telegraph.co.uk/football/2019/02/09/hugo-lloris-frances-world-cup-win-felt-empty/.

Defence is an Art. "N'golo Kante - World Cup 2018 - Best Defensive Skills (Re-Upload)." *YouTube*. July 24, 2018. https://www.youtube.com/watch?v=C4K2Bte39lc.

Delaney, Miguel. "Cruyff One of Football's Romantics." *ESPN*. October 4, 2013. https://www.espn.com/soccer/blog/espn-fc-united/68/post/1840878/johan-cruyff-one-of-footballs-romantics.

Deniran-Alleyne, Tashan. "The Story Behind the French Squad's Brilliant World Cup Tribute Song for Chelsea's N'Golo Kante." *football.london*. March 29, 2019. https://www.football.london/chelsea-fc/players/chelsea-news-ngolo-kante-song-14918057.

"Diego Valeri." *MLS*. 2019. https://www.mlssoccer.com/players/diego-valeri.

Dohrmann, George. "The Christian Pulisic Blueprint." *Bleacher Report*. June 7, 2017. https://bleacherreport.com/articles/2713937-the-christian-pulisic-blueprint.

Doyle, Paul. "N'Golo Kanté's Relentless Drive Takes Him to Historic Title Double." *The Guardian.* May 14, 2017. https://www .theguardian.com/football/2017/may/14/ngolo-kante-chelsea -back-to-back-titles-cantona-player-of-the-year.

"EAGER Chelsea News: Christian Pulisic 'Excited' to Play Alongside N'Golo Kante and 'Can't Wait to Meet Him.'" *talkSPORT.* May 13, 2019. https://talksport.com/football/542469 /chelsea-christian-pulisic-ngolo-kante/.

"Edin Džeko." *Wikipedia.* Accessed August 18, 2019. https://en .wikipedia.org/wiki/Edin_D%C5%BEeko.

"England National Football Team Statistics and Records: Appearances." *11v11.com.* 2019. https://www.11v11.com/teams /england/tab/stats/option/appearances/.

F2Freestylers - Ultimate Soccer Skills Channel. "Messi VS Ronaldo." *YouTube.* December 14, 2017. https://www.youtube.com /watch?v=y4p3YvXkLDM.

"FIFA World Player of the Year." *Wikipedia.* Accessed August 6, 2019. https://en.wikipedia.org/wiki/FIFA_World_Player_of_the_Year.

Fifield, Dominic. "Raheem Sterling Accuses Media of 'Fuelling Racism' after Alleged Abuse." *The Guardian.* December 9, 2018. https://www.theguardian.com/football/2018/dec/09/raheem -sterling-newspapers-fuelling-racism-alleged-abuse-chelsea.

"First Team Profiles - Maya Yoshida - Defender." *Southampton FC.* Accessed July 23, 2019. https://www.southamptonfc.com /first-team/maya-yoshida.

Fletcher, Paul. "N'Golo Kante: How Can Premier League Clubs Create Next Star?." *BBC.* March 29, 2017. https://www.bbc.com /sport/football/39248977.

Flin, Liam. "19 Facts You Did Not Know about Luka Modric." *Sportskeeda.* March 29, 2017. https://www.sportskeeda.com /football/19-facts-did-not-know-luka-modric/3.

Football Italia staff. "Bonucci: 'I wasn't going to celebrate.'" *Football Italia.* March 31, 2018. https://www.football-italia .net/119290/bonucci-i-wasnt-going-celebrate.

★ REFERENCES ★

"Football (Soccer)/The Leagues and Teams." *Wikibooks*. Accessed July 30, 2019. https://en.wikibooks.org/wiki/Football _(Soccer)/The_Leagues_and_Teams.

"Football Star Yaya Touré to Spotlight Illegal Wildlife Trade as UN Goodwill Ambassador | UN News." *UN News*. October 29, 2013. https://news.un.org/en/story/2013/10/454082-football-star -yaya-toure-spotlight-illegal-wildlife-trade-un-goodwill.

Forza Italian Football Staff. "Is Juventus' Arturo Vidal the Best Box-to-Box Midfielder in the World?" *Forza Italian Football*. March 17, 2013. https://forzaitalianfootball.com/2013/03/is -juventus-arturo-vidal-the-best-box-to-box-midfielder-in-the-world/.

Friend, Nick. "Raheem Sterling Honored with Award for Fight against Racism." *CNN*. April 26, 2019. https://edition.cnn.com /2019/04/25/football/raheem-sterling-racism-award-manchester -city-spt-intl/index.html.

"Goals, Stats for Messi & Cristiano Ronaldo." *messivsronaldo.net*. 2019. http://messivsronaldo.net/.

"Golden Consolation for Magical Modric." *FIFA.com*. July 15, 2018. https://www.fifa.com/worldcup/news/157-awards-piece -2986294.

Gómez, Roberto, and Harry De Cosemo. "Sergio Ramos' Love of Bullfighting." *MARCA*. Last modified May 25, 2016. https://www .marca.com/en/football/real-madrid/2016/05/25/57458251e2704e72 0c8b4588.html.

Gonzlez, Sergio G. "Twelve Things You Didn't Know About Virgil van Dijk." *MARCA*. December 28, 2017. https://www.marca.com /en/football/international-football/2017/12/28/5a452fd322601d 45358b45ae.html.

Grez, Matias. "Chelsea Bans Six Fans, One for Life, for Racist Abuse of Raheem Sterling." *CNN*. July 30, 2019. https://www.cnn .com/2019/07/30/football/chelsea-issue-bans-fans-racist-abuse -raheem-sterling-spt-intl/index.html.

Guardian sport. "Bastian Schweinsteiger Included in Germany's Provisional Euro 2016 Squad." *The Guardian*. May 17, 2016. https://www.theguardian.com/football/2016/may/17/bastian

★ REFERENCES ★

-schweinsteiger-germany-euro-2016-squad-manchester-united?
CMP=fb_a-football_b-gdnfootball.

Guardian sport. "The 100 Best Footballers in the World 2017." *The Guardian*. Accessed August 14, 2019. https://www.theguardian
.com/football/ng-interactive/2017/dec/19/the-100-best-footballers
-in-the-world-2017-interactive.

"'He Never Said No' — 11 Reasons Why It's Impossible Not to Love N'Golo Kanté." *Planet Football*. July 16, 2019. https://www
.planetfootball.com/quick-reads/11-reasons-why-its-impossible
-not-to-love-ngolo-kante/.

"Héctor Bellerín." *Wikipedia*. Accessed July 29, 2019. https://
en.wikipedia.org/wiki/H%C3%A9ctor_Beller%C3%ADn.

Heneage, Kristan. "A Decade On, Did David Beckham's Move to MLS Make a Difference?" *The Guardian*. January 11, 2017. https://
www.theguardian.com/football/blog/2017/jan/11/david-beckham
-la-galaxy-mls.

"Henry and Toure to Leave Barcelona." *CNN*. June 29, 2010.
http://edition.cnn.com/2010/SPORT/football/06/29/thierry.henry
.barcelona/index.html.

"Higuita: I Achieved Something Even Pele, Maradona and Messi Haven't." *FIFA.com.*April 24, 2018. https://www.fifa.com/worldcup
/news/higuita-achieved-pele-maradona-messi-havent.

Holyman, Ian. "Joshua Kimmich: The Origins of Bayern Munich's Next Superstar." *Bleacher Report*. November 13, 2016.
https://bleacherreport.com/articles/2675739-joshua-kimmich
-the-origins-of-bayern-munichs-next-superstar.

"How Jan Oblak Rose to Shine at Atlético." *UEFA Champions League*. May 3, 2016. https://www.uefa.com/uefachampionsleague
/news/newsid=2359881.html.

"Hugo Lloris." *Wikipedia*. Accessed July 1, 2019. https://en
.wikipedia.org/wiki/Hugo_Lloris.

"Hugo Lloris - Player Profile 19/20." *Transfermarkt*. 2019. https://
www.transfermarkt.us/hugo-lloris/profil/spieler/17965.

Hunter, Andy. "André Villas-Boas Defends Hugo Lloris Staying on with Head Injury." *The Guardian*. November 3, 2013. https://www

.theguardian.com/football/2013/nov/03/tottenham-villas-boas
-goal-record-everton.

"'If You Gave Me a Billion, I Wouldn't Sell Him' – PSG President Slaps Huge Price Tag On Kylian Mbappe." *talkSPORT*. Last modified June 7, 2018. https://talksport.com/football/376937 /if-you-gave-me-billion-euros-i-wouldnt-sell-him-psg-president -slaps-huge-price-tag-kylian/.

Ireland, Jack. "N'Golo Kante: How Chelsea Hit the Jackpot When They Signed the Diminutive Frenchman." *90min*. July 16, 2019. https://www.90min.com/posts/6412499-n-golo-kante-how-chelsea -hit-the-jackpot-when-they-signed-the-diminutive-frenchman.

"Is Bayern Munich Utility Man Joshua Kimmich the Most Versatile Player in World Football?" *Bundesliga*. September 12, 2018. https://www.bundesliga.com/en/news/Bundesliga/is-bayern -munich-utility-man-joshua-kimmich-the-most-versatile-player -in-world-football-512278.jsp.

"Jadon Sancho." *Wikipedia*. Accessed August 19, 2019. https:// en.wikipedia.org/wiki/Jadon_Sancho.

"Jadon Sancho: 10 Things on the Borussia Dortmund and England Record-Breaker." *Bundesliga*. November 16, 2018. https:// www.bundesliga.com/en/news/Bundesliga/jadon-sancho-10-things -on-the-borussia-dortmund-and-england-record-breaker-517140.jsp.

"Jan Oblak." *Wikipedia*. Accessed July 24, 2019. https://en .wikipedia.org/wiki/Jan_Oblak.

"Joshua Kimmich." *Wikipedia*. Accessed June 11, 2019. https:// en.wikipedia.org/wiki/Joshua_Kimmich.

"Joshua Kimmich - Titles & Victories." *Transfermarkt*. 2019. https://www.transfermarkt.us/joshua-kimmich/erfolge/spieler /161056.

"Kante Signs." *Chelsea FC*. July 16, 2016. https://www.chelseafc .com/en/news/2016/07/16/kante-signs.

Karen, Mattias. "Hector Bellerin Signs New Long-Term Contract at Arsenal." *ESPN*. November 21, 2016. https://www.espn.in/football /arsenal/story/3000954/hector-bellerin-signs-new-long-term -contract-at-arsenal.

★ REFERENCES ★

"Kevin De Bruyne." *Wikipedia.* Accessed August 10, 2019. https://en.wikipedia.org/wiki/Kevin_De_Bruyne.

Kimmich, Joshua. "Coming Up" *The Players' Tribune.* August 25, 2016. https://www.theplayerstribune.com/en-us/articles/joshua-kimmich-bayern-munich.

Krvavac, Fuad, Ondřej Zlámal, Philip Röber, and Paolo Menicucci. "How Brilliant Is Edin Džeko?" *UEFA Europa League.* March 23, 2019. https://www.uefa.com/uefaeuropaleague/news/newsid=2426669.html?iv=true.

Lee, Joon. "Kylian Mbappe: The Future of Football Is More Than the Future." *Bleacher Report.* July 23, 2018. https://bleacherreport.com/articles/2787035-kylian-mappe-france-world-football-power-50.

Lee, Joon. "The Boy Who Would Be King." *Bleacher Report.* December 6, 2017. https://bleacherreport.com/articles/2747750-the-boy-who-would-be-king.

"Leonardo Bonucci." *Wikipedia.* Accessed June 30, 2019. https://en.wikipedia.org/wiki/Leonardo_Bonucci.

Liverpool FC. "BEZZIES with Salah and Mane | Fastest? Best Haircut? Coffee or Lovren?" *YouTube.* September 6, 2018. https://www.youtube.com/watch?v=jRsqG5E_SgQ&t=337s.

Longman, Jere. "WORLD CUP '94; Awake, America! Let Soccer Ring." *The New York Times.* June 12, 1994. https://www.nytimes.com/1994/06/12/sports/world-cup-94-awake-america-let-soccer-ring.html.

Maguire, Ken. "Sadio Mane Was the 'Quiet Kid' with the Superstar Talent." *StarTribune.* June 8, 2018. http://www.startribune.com/sadio-mane-was-the-quiet-kid-with-the-superstar-talent/484972131/?refresh=true.

"Manchester United Greatest XI." *The Telegraph.* January 29, 2016. https://www.telegraph.co.uk/football/2016/01/29/manchester-united-players-best-11-of-all-time/peter-schmeichel-celebrating/.

★ REFERENCES ★

Mannion, Damian. "Take It, It's Yours: Olivier Giroud Confirms N'Golo Kante Was Too Shy to Hold the World Cup Trophy After France Beat Croatia." *talkSPORT*. August 21, 2018. https://talksport.com/football/413354/giroud-chelsea-team-mate-kante-shy-world-cup/.

"Maya Yoshida." *Wikipedia*. Accessed June 26, 2019. https://en.wikipedia.org/wiki/Maya_Yoshida.

"Mbappe Shakes Off Pele Comparisons After Stunning Brace." *RTÉ*. Last modified June 30, 2018. https://www.rte.ie/sport/world-cup-2018/2018/0630/974415-mbappe-shakes-off-pele-comparisons-after-stunning-brace/.

McDonnell, David. "The Story of Virgil van Dijk: From Pot Washer to the World's Most-Expensive Defender in Just 10 Years." *Mirror*. January 3, 2018. https://www.mirror.co.uk/sport/football/news/story-virgil-van-dijk-pot-11791844.

McLaughlin, Eliott C. "Brand Beckham: Persona More Than Play Helped Popularize Soccer in America." *CNN*. May 17, 2013. https://www.cnn.com/2013/05/16/us/beckham-american-impact/.

McNulty, Phil. "Ecuador 2-2 England." *BBC*. June 4, 2014. https://www.bbc.com/sport/football/27383424.

Menicucci, Paolo, and Ben Gladwell. "Italy's 'BBC' Spell out Programme for Solidity." *UEFA Euro 2016*. June 9, 2016. https://web.archive.org/web/20160613080653/http://www.uefa.com/uefaeuro/news/newsid=2372826.html.

"Mesut Özil." *Wikipedia*. Accessed August 11, 2019. https://en.wikipedia.org/wiki/Mesut_%C3%96zil.

"Mohamed Salah - Titles & Victories." *Transfermarkt*. 2019. https://www.transfermarkt.com/mohamed-salah/erfolge/spieler/148455.

"Mohamed Salah." *Wikipedia*. Accessed August 13, 2019. https://en.wikipedia.org/wiki/Mohamed_Salah.

Morgan, Tom, and Jon West. "Hugo Lloris 'Wholeheartedly' Apologises after Drink-Driving Charge." *The Telegraph*. August 24, 2018. https://www.telegraph.co.uk/football/2018/08/24/hugo-lloris-spurs-goalkeer-charged-drink-driving/.

"N'Golo Kanté - Player Profile 19/20." *Transfermarkt*. 2019.
https://www.transfermarkt.us/ngolo-kante/profil/spieler/225083.

Nazareth, Danny. "5 Things About Christian Pulisic That You
Didn't Know." *Sportskeeda*. Accessed September 17, 2019. https://
www.sportskeeda.com/football/5-things-about-christian-pulisic
-that-you-didn-t-know-sstl/5.

Oh My Goal. "René Higuita: The Craziest Goalkeeper in History!"
YouTube. December 8, 2018. https://www.youtube.com/watch
?v=kFbH34tYHRs.

"Paris Saint-Germain Cleared of Breaking Uefa's FFP Rules."
The Guardian. June 13, 2018. https://www.theguardian.com
/football/2018/jun/13/psg-uefa-ffp-raise-funds-rules.

PA Sport. "Birthday Boys N'Golo Kante and Dimitri Payet Help
France to Victory." *Eurosport*. March 29, 2016. https://www
.eurosport.co.uk/football/birthday-boys-n-golo-kante-and-dimitri
-payet-help-france-to-victory_sto5415101/story.shtml.

"Peter Schmeichel." *24celebs.com*. July 3, 2018. https://24celebs
.com/celebrity/58034-peter-schmeichel.html.

"Peter Schmeichel." *Wikipedia*. Accessed July 2, 2019. https://
en.wikipedia.org/wiki/Peter_Schmeichel.

Pirks, Natalie. "Raheem Sterling: Liverpool Forward Turns
Down New Deal." *BBC*. April 1, 2015. https://www.bbc.com/sport
/football/32149613.

Planinšič, Borut. "With 'This Little One Is Better than Me' It Began
[Translated from Slovenian]." *Vecer.com*. May 19, 2018. https://www
.vecer.com/s-ta-mali-je-boljsi-od-mene-se-je-zacelo-6474456.

Prince-Wright, Joe. "Why Johan Cruyff Was the Most Influential
Man in Soccer History." *NBC Sports*. March 24, 2016. https://soccer
.nbcsports.com/2016/03/24/why-johan-cruyff-was-the-most
-influential-man-in-soccer-history/.

Ramos, Sergio. "My Story." *Sergio Ramos*. 2019. https://www
.sergioramos.com/conoce-mi-historia/.

Ramos, Sergio. "Reaching the 100-Appearances Mark Against
Sevilla." *Sergio Ramos*. 2007. https://www.sergioramos.com
/en/100-partidos-en-liga/.

"Real Madrid's Sergio Ramos Drops Copa Del Rey Trophy Off Bus." *The Telegraph.* April 21, 2011. https://www.telegraph.co.uk/sport/sportvideo/footballvideo/8465404/Real-Madrids-Sergio-Ramos-drops-Copa-del-Rey-trophy-off-bus.html.

Reddy, Melissa. "Sadio Mane's Story: How I Went From Torn Boots and Shorts on Senegal's Streets to a Liverpool Sensation." *Goal.com.* 2016. https://www.goal.com/en/news/2466/goal-50/2016/11/08/29293582/sadio-manes-story-how-i-went-from-torn-boots-and-shorts-on.

Rico, Francisco. "El Homenaje a Su Amigo Antonio Puerta: Por Qué Sergio Ramos Usa El Dorsal 15 En La Selección De España." *Goal.com.* July 1, 2018. https://www.goal.com/es-ar/noticias/el-homenaje-a-su-amigo-por-que-sergio-ramos-usa-el-dorsal-15/faeqoyu3re1t186ocmnouke2m.

Rob. "Hugo Lloris Biography." *Playerswiki.com.* Last modified July 8, 2018. https://playerswiki.com/hugo-lloris.

"Sadio Mané - Titles & Victories." *Transfermarkt.* 2019. https://www.transfermarkt.us/sadio-mane/erfolge/spieler/200512.

"Saint-Lloris, Priez Pour Nous!" *Football 365.* July 10, 2011. https://www.football365.fr/saint-lloris-priez-pour-nous-1199191.html.

"Sergio Ramos - Titles & Victories." *Transfermarkt.* 2019. https://www.transfermarkt.com/sergio-ramos/erfolge/spieler/25557.

"Sergio Ramos Joins Real Madrid for €27 Million." *thinkSPAIN.* September 1, 2005. https://www.thinkspain.com/news-spain/9451/sergio-ramos-joins-real-madrid-for-27-million.

Sherman, Justin. "The Making of Luka Modrić from War-Torn Croatia to the World's Best Midfielder." *These Football Times.* September 10, 2017. https://thesefootballtimes.co/2017/10/09/the-making-of-luka-modric-from-war-torn-croatia-to-the-worlds-best-midfielder/.

Smith, Alex. "Hugo Lloris Reveals Becoming a Professional Footballer Was His Second Choice as He Wanted to Star In Another Sport." *Mirror.* November 1, 2017. https://www.mirror.co.uk/sport/football/news/hugo-lloris-reveals-becoming-professional-11448749.

Smith, Andy. "How Did Borussia Dortmund Star Christian Pulisic Make It Into the European Big Leagues?" *Bundesliga*. November 20, 2018. https://www.bundesliga.com/en/news/Bundesliga/how -did-christian-pulisic-make-it-into-the-european-big-leagues -dortmund-512258.jsp.

Smith, Andy. "Precocious Christian Pulisic Continues to Break Records with Borussia Dortmund." *Bundesliga*. September 15, 2016. https://www.bundesliga.com/en/news/Bundesliga/noblmd3 -another-record-for-rising-star-christian-pulisic-borussia-dortmund.jsp.

Smith, Rory. "Yaya and Kolo Toure Bound by Family Ties to Manchester City." *The Telegraph*. July 23, 2010. https://www .telegraph.co.uk/sport/football/teams/manchester-city/7907545 /Yaya-and-Kolo-Toure-bound-by-family-ties-to-Manchester -City.html.

Sobhani, Kiyan. "The Making of N'Golo Kante, By Those Who Witnessed His Incredible Rise." *FourFourTwo*. March 20, 2017. https://www.fourfourtwo.com/us/features/making-ngolo-kante -those-who-witnessed-his-incredible-rise?page=0%2C1.

"Soccer-First Female Referee to Officiate Super Cup Not Afraid of Intense Spotlight." *Reuters*. August 13, 2019. https://uk.reuters .com/article/champions-referee/soccer-first-female-referee-to -officiate-super-cup-no-afraid-of-intense-spotlight-idUKL8N2594JL.

"Southampton Sign Maya Yoshida, Japan's Olympic Captain." *BBC*. August 30, 2012. https://www.bbc.com/sport /football/19426865.

Southwick, Andrew. "Aberdeen 2-1 Celtic." *BBC*. February 25, 2014. https://www.bbc.com/sport/football/25892139.

Spencer, Jamie. "Sadio Mane Reveals Remarkable Story That Saw Him Run Away From Home at 15 to Make It as a Footballer." *90min*. January 3, 2018. https://www.90min.com/posts/5936555-sadio -mane-reveals-remarkable-story-that-saw-him-run-away-from -home-at-15-to-make-it-as-a-footballer.

Sport, BT. "When Mo Salah Met Gary Lineker." *YouTube*. May 31, 2019. https://www.youtube.com/watch?v=panAw8lDGkw.

Stanton, John, and Ashleigh Jackson. "Premier League 2015-16: The Season That Defied Expectations." *BBC*. May 17, 2016. https://www.bbc.com/sport/football/36255713.

"Sterling Reaches 50 Premier League Goals with Arsenal Strike." *Goal.com*. August 12, 2018. https://www.goal.com/en/news/sterling-reaches-50-premier-league-goals-with-arsenal-strike/ulzk24xys30419nb4wlqita6u.

Sterling, Raheem. "In the Shadow of Wembley." *The Players' Tribune*. July 3, 2018. https://www.theplayerstribune.com/en-us/videos/raheem-sterling-in-the-shadow-of-wembley.

Sterling, Raheem. "It Was All a Dream." *The Players' Tribune*. June 21, 2018. https://www.theplayerstribune.com/en-us/articles/raheem-sterling-england-it-was-all-a-dream.

Storer, Tom. "Bellerin Mature Enough to Come Back Stronger for Arsenal - Emery." *Goal.com*. January 23, 2019. https://www.goal.com/en/news/bellerin-mature-enough-to-come-back-stronger-for-arsenal/f8865e3f8pyg151fhuhph128y.

Taylor, Daniel. "France Seal Second World Cup Triumph with 4-2 Win Over Brave Croatia." *The Guardian*. July 15, 2018. https://www.theguardian.com/football/2018/jul/15/france-croatia-world-cup-final-match-report.

"Ten Things You Didnt Know about Raheem Sterling." *Manchester City FC*. September 4, 2015. https://www.mancity.com/news/first-team/first-team-news/2015/september/ten-things-you-didnt-know-about-raheem-sterling.

Terreur, Kristof. "Kevin De Bruyne: The Stubborn Boy Who Developed Into a World Beater." *The Guardian*. October 20, 2017. https://www.theguardian.com/football/2017/oct/20/kevin-de-bruyne-stubborn--world-beater.

The Sun. "Virgil van Dijk has Revealed that He Suffered a Burst Appendix When He Was 17 that Nearly Claimed His Life." *Fox Sports*. March 24, 2019. https://www.foxsports.com.au/football/premier-league/virgil-van-dijk-has-revealed-that-he-suffered-a-burst-appendix-when-he-was-17-that-nearly-claimed-his-life/news-story/3da820bc0270a1259cf8bae2f3f854b1.

★ REFERENCES ★

"Thorgan Hazard: 10 Things You Might Not Know About the Belgium and Gladbach Star." *Bundesliga.* July 14, 2018. https:// www.bundesliga.com/en/news/Bundesliga/thorgan-hazard-10 -things-about-the-belgium-and-monchengladbach-star-461337.jsp.

Thorogood, James. "The New Faces of the German National Team." *Deutsche Welle.* March 15, 2019. https://www.dw.com/en /the-new-faces-of-the-german-national-team/a-47938812.

"Tim Howard." *Wikipedia.* Accessed July 3, 2019. https://en .wikipedia.org/wiki/Tim_Howard.

"Top 26 Amazing Facts You Need to Know About Mo Salah." *Great Performers Academy.* 2019. https://greatperformersacademy .com/motivation/top-26-amazing-facts-you-need-to-know-about -mo-salah.

vannyhenrico. "Hugo Lloris Childhood Story Plus Untold Biography Facts." *LifeBogger.* February 1, 2018. https://lifebogger .com/hugo-lloris-childhood-story-plus-untold-biography-facts/.

vannyhenrico. "Sergio Ramos Childhood Story Plus Untold Biography Facts." *LifeBogger.* October 19, 2017. https://lifebogger .com/sergio-ramos-childhood-story-plus-untold-biography-facts/.

vannyhenrico. "Yaya Toure Childhood Story Plus Untold Biography Facts." *LifeBogger.* March 29, 2019. https://lifebogger .com/yaya-toure-childhood-story-plus-untold-biography-facts/.

Verschueren, Gianni. "Leonardo Bonucci Responds to Instagram Troll Who Wished Death on His Children." *Bleacher Report.* September 14, 2018. https://bleacherreport.com/articles/2795710 -leonardo-bonucci-responds-to-instagram-troll-who-wished -death-on-his-children.

Veselica, Lajla. "Modric, from Child Refugee to Croatia's World Cup Captain." *Chicago Tribune.* May 29, 2018. https://www .chicagotribune.com/90minutes/ct-90mins-modric-20180529 -story.html.

Vice Sports. "Das American: Christian Pulisic's Spectacular Rise." *YouTube.* November 9, 2016. https://www.youtube.com /watch?v=bbiY0Sk1G0g.

Vickery, Tim. "The Legacy of Rene Higuita." *BBC*. February 1, 2010. https://www.bbc.co.uk/blogs/timvickery/2010/02/the_legacy_of _rene_higuita.html.

"Video Sadio Mane Goals vs Aston Villa 2015 – Fastest League Hat Trick – Three Goals in 3 Minutes Shane Long Goal." *Soccer Blog | Football News, Reviews, Quizzes.* May 16, 2015. http://www .soccer-blogger.com/2015/05/16/video-sadio-mane-goals-vs-aston -villa-fastest-league-hat-trick-three-goals-in-3-minutes-shane-long -goal-southampton-6-1-aston-villa/.

"Virgil Van Dijk - Player Profile 19/20." *Transfermarkt.* 2019. https://www.transfermarkt.us/virgil-van-dijk/profil/spieler/139208.

"Virgil van Dijk: Liverpool Apologise & End Interest in Southampton Defender." *BBC.* June 7, 2017. https://www.bbc.com /sport/football/40194862.

"Virgil van Dijk Wants to Be 'a Legend of Liverpool' - in-Depth Wide-Ranging BBC Interview." *BBC.* February 21, 2019. https:// www.bbc.com/sport/football/47283936.

Wahl, Grant. "HOLLYWOOD ENDING." *Vault.* November 28, 2011. https://www.si.com/vault/2011/11/28/106135817/hollywood -ending.

Wallace, Sam. "Eden Hazard: My Family Would Make a Great Five-a-Side Team." *The Independent.* December 8, 2012. https:// www.independent.co.uk/incoming/eden-hazard-my-family -would-make-a-great-five-a-side-team-8393517.html.

Williams, Richard. "Johan Cruyff: The Revolutionary Who Changed How the World Saw Football." *The Guardian.* March 24, 2016. https://www.theguardian.com/football/2016/mar/24/johan-cruyff -revolutionary-changed-football-richard-williams.

Williams, Tom. "Selfless Sadio Mane Finds Home Away from Home Within Liverpool Collective." *Bleacher Report.* September 12, 2018. https://bleacherreport.com/articles/2795243-selfless-sadio -mane-finds-home-away-from-home-within-liverpool-collective.

Wilson, Jonathan. "Tottenham's Hugo Lloris Is Premier League's Supreme Sweeper-Keeper." *The Guardian.* February 13, 2014. https://www.theguardian.com/football/blog/2014/feb/13 /tottenham-hugo-lloris-premier-league-sweeper-keeper.

Wilson, Paul. "Yaya Touré: Manchester City 'Is a Story Waiting to Be Written.'" *The Guardian.* October 22, 2011. https://www .theguardian.com/football/2011/oct/22/yaya-toure-manchester-city.

"Yaya Toure Speaks out on Racism: The Worst Thing Was Having to Play Again." *MARCA.* April 2, 2019. https://www .marca.com/en/football/international-football/2019/04/02/ 5ca34163ca4741f72f8b4647.html.

"Yaya Touré." *Wikipedia.* Accessed July 23, 2019. https://en .wikipedia.org/wiki/Yaya_Tour%C3%A9.

Acknowledgments

To my family, thank you for allowing me the time to do this project and for your support in the process. You are the greatest soccer travel posse I could ever ask for.

Thank you to all the supporters, fans, soccer nerds, and friends who contributed to my lifelong accumulation of soccer knowledge, but especially to the kids who contributed their advice and support to this book: Raphael Jotzke, Jonah Wilke-Shapiro, Jakob Welch, and Miguel Gosnell.

Thank you to my editor, David Lytle, for being so excited about this project and for keeping me from completely flipping out about deadlines, and to the rest of the team at Callisto for the opportunity to write a dream project.

Thanks to my parents for telling me that it was great that I went to the World Cup in 1998 because I'd have kids and wouldn't be able to go in 2002, thus ensuring that all my children would be planned around World Cups. Thanks to both my parents and my in-laws for all that you do to support our soccer life, from taking care of kids to watching the house. We are so lucky to have your support.

On May 17, 2018, I was in a car accident that left me with a mild form of traumatic brain injury called postconcussive syndrome. I had trouble

doing anything but lying in a quiet, dark room. This book would not have been possible without my occupational therapist Aaron Aamodt (despite him supporting the Seattle Sounders) and the rest of the amazing staff at On With Life Brain Rehab. I'm so grateful to you all for showing me the way to put my life back together.

Finally, to the people in my soccer family of supporters, thank you for helping create the grand adventure that soccer is for our family. Whether we met in KKIFE, AO, Charlie Company, Timbers Army, Sammers, or Red Army, you are some of the finest, most supportive, and rivetingly interesting people I've ever met. It's an honor and a pleasure to stand and sing with you.

About the Author

For the past 26 years, Tanya Keith has traveled around the world following US Soccer. First as a referee, then as a coach, player, supporter, and parent, she has experienced American soccer from all angles. She writes about some of her experiences on her blog, SoccerFamilyStyle.com.

Across the United States and through 14 countries, Tanya has watched US Soccer supporters grow from a small group that couldn't fill a single stadium section in the early '90s to filling stadiums near and far with love for both the women's and men's teams. Her first book, *Passionate Soccer Love*, is a memoir of her first 20 years of traveling adventure to follow the rise of US Soccer around the world.

Tanya lives in Des Moines, Iowa, where she does her level best to not startle the Midwesterners with her Jersey girl verve. She is a proud supporter of the Des Moines Menace and the Timbers Army Heartland Regiment. She lives with her husband, Doug, and their hat trick of children: Aviva, Raphael, and Iolana. When she is not watching or writing about soccer, you will find her making ceramics or stained glass, or renovating Victorian and turn-of-the-century homes with her company, Hat Trick Renovation.

CPSIA information can be obtained
at www.ICGtesting.com
Printed in the USA
LVHW020241231119
638246LV00006B/180/P

9 781646 112128